Frederick Milnes Edge

Major-General McClellan and the Campaign on the Yorktown Peninsula

Frederick Milnes Edge

Major-General McClellan and the Campaign on the Yorktown Peninsula

ISBN/EAN: 9783337427696

Printed in Europe, USA, Canada, Australia, Japan

Cover: Foto ©Suzi / pixelio.de

More available books at **www.hansebooks.com**

MAJOR-GENERAL McCLELLAN

AND

THE CAMPAIGN ON THE YORKTOWN PENINSULA.

BY

FREDERICK MILNES EDGE,

Author of 'Slavery Doomed,' 'Destruction of the American Carrying Trade,'
'President Lincoln's Successor,' 'The Alabama and the Kearsarge,' &c.
and late Special Correspondent of the *Morning Star* with the
Armies of the United States.

WITH A MAP OF THE PENINSULA

DRAWN EXPRESSLY FOR THIS WORK

BY JAMES WYLD, GEOGRAPHER TO THE QUEEN.

LONDON:
TRÜBNER & CO., 60 PATERNOSTER ROW.
1865.

LONDON
PRINTED BY SPOTTISWOODE AND CO.
NEW-STREET SQUARE

CONTENTS.

CHAPTER I.
INTRODUCTORY 1

CHAPTER II.
DISAPPEARANCE OF THE CONFEDERATES FROM THE LINES OF MANASSAS 10

CHAPTER III.
EMBARKATION OF THE ARMY OF THE POTOMAC FOR THE PENINSULA . 18

CHAPTER IV.
ADVANCE OF GENERAL M'DOWELL'S CORPS UPON WARRINGTON JUNCTION 37

CHAPTER V.
AMERICAN IRON-CLADS 49

CHAPTER VI.
A GENERAL VIEW OF AFFAIRS 58

CHAPTER VII.
THE YORKTOWN PENINSULA . . . 64

CHAPTER VIII.
IN FRONT OF YORKTOWN 73

CHAPTER IX.
EVACUATION OF YORKTOWN 80

CONTENTS.

CHAPTER X.
BATTLE OF WEST POINT, VA 87

CHAPTER XI.
THE MARCH UP THE PENINSULA 97

CHAPTER XII.
BATTLE OF WILLIAMSBURG 106

CHAPTER XIII.
WHITE HOUSE 108

CHAPTER XIV.
THE LINES OF THE CHICKAHOMINY 126

CHAPTER XV.
BATTLE OF HANOVER COURT HOUSE . . . 138

CHAPTER XVI.
BATTLE OF FAIR OAKS 141

CHAPTER XVII.
IN SIGHT OF RICHMOND 145

CHAPTER XVIII.
ON THE CENTRE 171

CHAPTER XIX.
THE RETREAT 188
CONCLUSION 200

GENERAL McCLELLAN.

CHAPTER I.

INTRODUCTORY.

The unparalleled uprising of the American people in the spring of 1861, and the unanimous resolve of the Governments and Legislatures of all the Northern States to support the newly-elected President in his opposition to Secession, swept away for a time every party distinction, and proved conclusively to the world that the Free North was an unit in defence of the integrity of the Republic. Foremost amongst those who offered their services and lives to the Federal Government in defence of the Union, were the recognised chiefs of the Democratic party; and, for the moment, there was every prospect that party distinctions had ceased to exist, and minor questions of domestic policy had given way to the overwhelming necessity of subduing the rebellion.

The leaders of the Democratic and Republican parties, the ablest statesmen in the North, the President himself and his advisers, failed at the outset to appreciate the magnitude of the crisis. It took many months of half-measures, and frequent disasters, to raise them to the height of the situation; whilst the vast mass of the citizens urged them forward by every means in their power, and furnished an example of self-sacrificing patriotism which no other people in modern times has equalled. When, on the memorable 15th day of April, 1861, President Lincoln issued his proclamation calling for 75,000 volunteers, there was a feeling of disappointment throughout the North; for almost every man felt disposed to lay aside his business to avenge the insult to his country's flag at Fort Sumter. The legislature of the State of New York responded immediately to the President's call, by voting 30,000 men and 3,000,000 dollars to put down the rebellion, and other States followed her example with similar enthusiasm. When, again, the new Secretary of the Treasury sought for monetary aid from the banks of New York and other great financial centres, and met with hesitation or refusal from the various boards of directors, the shareholders themselves convened meetings and compelled those directors, their servants, to aid and encourage the Government to the utmost extent of their ability. Later in the year, after the crushing disaster on the Plains of Manassas, when President Lincoln demanded 400,000 men 'for three years, or the war,' Congress responded by voting him 500,000, which the people increased to 700,000, and would have carried on to a million had not the Government put a stop suddenly to the volunteering. The whole body of the citizens, in fine, with all their time-honoured political leaders, advanced the President and Congress alike in the energy of their patriotism. Nor was this enthusiasm and self-devotion merely confined to the men; in all the cities, towns, villages, and hamlets of the Union-loving North, the women met in each other's houses, working from morn to night, to provide clothing and hospital necessaries for their husbands, sons, and brothers in the field. Party organisations seemed for ever obliterated, every political difference or shade being swallowed up in the universal cry, 'We, the people of the United States, are resolved to crush this rebellion, whatever may be the cost in time, or treasure, or blood.'

All the recognised leaders of the Democratic party—such men as Dickinson, Johnson, Dix, and Butler—were heartily co-operating with the Government in its efforts to enforce the national authority. So unexpected a result utterly surprised the Southern rebels, for they had calculated upon a divided North through the very instrumentality of this Democratic party, which had hitherto shown itself so subservient to Southern policy and interests. Southern astonishment, however, did not give birth to despair. Thoroughly well-informed by certain politicians in the free States upon the extent and depth of popular sentiment; knowing the hold taken by 'Democratic' organisation upon the foreign element in the great cities of the North, and convinced that the war they had commenced would be a long one, they resolved to reconstruct the party with new leaders. Those politicians of the Northern democracy who held aloof from the Government and viewed the universal uprising of their fellow-citizens in stolid silence, if not with treasonable disgust, were of too small calibre and restricted influence to be used except in a secondary capacity. It was necessary to select some person around whom the broken and demoralised democracy might rally, and a secret meeting was held for this purpose in the city of Baltimore, in the early part of the month of June, 1861, at which self-appointed representatives of the Northern democracy and Southern delegates met in council. The opinions there enunciated by the latter were earnestly favourable to a restoration of the Union on the former pro-slavery basis, but with the exclusion of the New England States; this assurance being obviously motived by the necessity of quieting the scruples of their Northern coadjutors. The selection of a Democratic chieftain proved, however, to be a matter of great difficulty, until it was suggested that, in view of the warlike tone of public sentiment in the free States, an army officer should be chosen. This proposition was received with marks of approbation by all present. The suggestion was one that all there could appreciate at its full value, for the United States Military Academy, at West Point, was intensely 'democratic' in its politics, and had long been under Southern tutelage and careful supervision. During the previous eight years Mr. Jefferson Davis, first as Secretary of War under President Pierce, and subsequently as Chairman of the Standing Committee of the Senate on military affairs during Mr. Buchanan's administration—had enjoyed ample opportunities for becoming fully acquainted with the abilities and political tendencies of the young men there educated; and, on the other hand, in selecting an army officer for training as their future standard-bearer, the Northern democracy might thereby be enabled to turn the warlike enthusiasm of the Free States to their own party-interest and profit. The meeting adjourned, to re-assemble in a week, the interim being devoted by the members to making enquiries as to the most available officer for their choice. With but three dissentients, Captain George B. McClellan was the officer selected; and the arguments used in favour of his adoption were immediately conducive towards making the choice unanimous. As the former *protégé* of Mr. Davis, he would of course obtain the suffrages of the Southern representatives, whilst his antecedents and personal qualifications would naturally commend him to Northern favour. He was quite unknown in the political world, but his relatives and associates were staunch supporters of the Democratic faith. He was a native of Pennsylvania, and he might win back that important State to the Democratic ranks; whilst his business relations with the West, as engineer of the Illinois Central Railroad, would insure him supporters in that section.

On the 20th of June, Captain McClellan took command of the Union forces in the mountainous region of Western Virginia, and the Democratic newspapers of the North forthwith commenced to put his name prominently before the country, and to recommend him as the ablest and most promising officer in the army. Although never seen upon any battlefield during the engagement, the rapid successes of such subordinates as Rosecrans were immediately ascribed to him; and when he issued his flaming theatrical proclamation announcing that Western Virginia was cleared of the rebels, the whole body of the Northern people were easily taught to believe that the safety of the Republic would be secure in his hands. A strong pressure was forthwith brought to bear upon the Government at Washington; Lieutenant-General Scott was animadverted upon constantly in the Democratic press, as too old for the onerous duties pressing on his attention; and where argument failed, ridicule was brought to bear. President Lincoln manfully resisted this growing pressure until the night of Sunday, July 21st, when the terrible and unexpected repulse of the Union army at Bull Run forced him to surrender his scruples, and McClellan was telegraphed to the same night to come immediately to Washington.

I had just then arrived in the United States, and, on my way to the capital, rode in the same train with the new commander of the Army of the Potomac from Philadelphia to Washington. He was accompanied by two friends, Major Stoneman (now Major-General) of the United States army, and Judge Key of Ohio; and a private carriage was added to the train for their convenience. All three were in plain clothes, except that General McClellan wore a French *képi* cap. The journey was full of incident, it being known to all aboard who was in the train, and he was lustily cheered by the citizens at the different stations along the route, and on two occasions was forced to address the assembled crowd. When the train was slowing off, as we neared Baltimore, the General exchanged his *képi* for the Major's 'wide-awake,' and the three travellers leaped from the train while it was still in motion, and walked quickly through the city to the Washington terminus. The precaution was judicious, for the 'plug uglies' and 'blood tubs' of that terrible Baltimore might have impeded his journey to the capital.

Washington was in a fearful condition on his arrival. The disastrous retreat from Bull Run had filled the city with demoralised and riotous soldiery, and it was scarcely safe for unarmed persons to walk the streets, even in broad daylight. Within forty-eight hours all this disorder disappeared as though by magic; few volunteers were seen away from barracks or east of the Potomac; a determined provost guard patrolled the city constantly, and even general officers were arrested who could not produce a pass. Naturally enough, McClellan received the credit of all this rapid improvement, and yet it was entirely due to the advice given him through letter on his arrival, by an intimate friend, in whose judgment he had confidence.

Not a single detail of this advice was modified or changed; but McClellan is justly entitled to credit for the energy with which he carried out his friend's recommendation. All must regret that similar energy was not displayed by him in the subsequent duties of the campaign.

General McClellan has gained much reputation for his organisation of the Army of the Potomac under the second call for 500,000 volunteers; but it does not follow that a good drill officer will make a competent commander in presence of the enemy. The credit of that organisation really belongs to his subordinates, and notably to General Seth Williams—a quiet, unassuming officer, who has held the position of Adjutant-General of the Army of the Potomac under M'Dowell, McClellan himself, Pope, Burnside, Hooker, Meade, and still continues to hold it. McClellan had very little to do with the shaping of that army beyond two or three reviews, and these were given in compliment to foreign notabilities rather than for any purposes of instruction. I was best acquainted with the division under General Franklin, having passed nearly all my time with it from the period of McClellan's arrival at Washington until his departure for the Yorktown peninsula, and I recollect his reviewing it on a single occasion only. The duty of shaping raw recruits into soldiers was left to colonels, brigadiers, and division commanders; the volunteers saw little of those movements which are necessary to produce effectiveness *as an army*; and it was a subject of general complaint, that beyond brigade-drill they were trained to nothing else. This fault was apparent throughout the entire campaign, *corps* and division generals fighting their commands single-handed, without let, hindrance, or advice from the Commander-in-Chief. Thus Hooker struggled alone during a whole day against the rebel army at Williamsburg, until Kearny came to his aid *without orders*; and at Fair Oaks, Sumner threw his *corps* across the Chickahominy, and retrieved a terrible disaster *without McClellan's knowledge.*

The plans of the Democratic party were most ably seconded by the newspapers in its interest. Within a few weeks of the new Commander-in-Chief arriving in Washington, the troops began to regard him as something almost more than human; they were taught by their papers to speak of him as the 'Young Napoleon,' 'Little Mac,' &c., and the most extraordinary stories were gravely published as to his plans and personal movements. By some means or other, only those papers which professed fealty to the Democratic party, and the most grovelling adulation of the General, found circulation amongst the troops. The *New York Herald* and *Philadelphia Inquirer*, in the Eastern armies; the *Chicago Times* and *Cincinnati Enquirer* in the Western, deluged the camps; whilst such papers as the New York *Tribune* and *Times*, the *Chicago Journal* and *Tribune*, could with difficulty be bought, for the news-agents would not bring them into camp. It was by such means that McClellan's reputation was built up in the first instance; and the feeling in his favour was still further increased when these Democratic organs reiterated from day to day that the Government was withholding reinforcements from his army, so as to ensure his defeat and damage him politically. But Americans are essentially a practical people; and they came to understand, after the Peninsula campaign, that all this newspaper hullabaloo was merely made in view of Presidential purposes.

McClellan's position in Washington, from July 1861 to the spring of '62, was rather that of a Dictator than of a mere General. His house on President's Square was the real 'White House;' Senators and Members of Congress waited in his ante-chambers, and crowds hung around his door. On the 1st of Nov. 1861, Lieutenant-General Scott resigned the command-in-chief of the Union armies, and the young captain of engineers of seven months previous vaulted into the position. The Baltimore plot was in fair way of realisation.

Across the Potomac, on the lines of Arlington Heights and Alexandria, 150,000 men threw up forts, redoubts, and earthworks, and were carefully drilled by their own officers; while the 'Young Napoleon' passed his time pleasantly in the capital. There was occasional picket-shooting 'in the season,' but no semblance of active operations against the enemy, who were pressing them almost into the river. Until September the 28th, the rebel flag flaunted defiantly in sight of the Capitol itself.

But the citizens and Government at last grew tired of the eternal refrain, 'All quiet on the Potomac,' and the 'Young Napoleon' received an order to move on with such emphasis that he dared not refuse obedience to the mandate.

CHAPTER II.

DISAPPEARANCE OF THE CONFEDERATES FROM THE LINES OF MANASSAS.

WASHINGTON: March 13.

WE have apparently lost sight of the enemy. Some suppose the Confederate army has fallen back towards Richmond, others assert that a considerable portion of it has gone to reinforce General Joseph Johnston in the northern part of the State, whilst many express their fears that Burnside will be overwhelmed by it before succour can reach him. McClellan is slowly creeping into Lower Virginia in great force, and Banks has occupied Winchester, without opposition; but whether the former or the latter will first attack or be attacked it is impossible to say. Perhaps McClellan is merely taking up a position to prevent the retreat of Johnston's army upon Richmond, and when this is effected the rebels will be taken between his forces and those of Banks. I received a very broad hint to this effect a few days ago, and am daily expecting another which shall decide whether I attach myself for the present to the army of the General-in-Chief or to that of his subordinate. I do not think McClellan will attack the main body of the Confederates to the southward while their northern army threatens his rear, and have therefore remained in Washington until events further develope themselves. A few hours will carry me to either of the two points, and I shall thus be enabled to witness the first engagement.

There is a stronger outcry than ever against McClellan for letting the enemy slip away from Manassas. The general opinion is that he has been fooled by the wily foe, and the only parties disposed to show confidence in him and his plans are the West Point officers, who seem to think that a word against him is a reflection, not complimentary, upon themselves.

The following order was issued on Tuesday last:— 'Major-General McClellan having personally taken the field at the head of the army of the Potomac, *until otherwise ordered*, he is relieved from the command of the other military departments, he retaining command of the department of the Potomac.' The words in italics certainly seem to convey a threat. The same order contains also the following:—' Ordered also, that the country west of the department of the Potomac and east of the department of the Mississippi' (that is to say, from a line drawn due north and south through Knoxville, Tennessee) ' be a military department, to be called the Mountain Department, and that the same be commanded by Major-General Fremont.' This region includes the extreme mountainous districts of Western Virginia, Kentucky, and Tennessee, and does not afford the Pathfinder much field for action. General Halleck now commands on both sides of the Mississippi river, Hunter and Buell being ordered to report henceforward to him. The order winds up as follows:— ' All the commanders of departments, after the receipt of this order by them respectively, will report severally and directly to the Secretary of War, and prompt, full, and frequent reports will be expected of all and each of them.

'ABRAHAM LINCOLN.'

The main army of the Confederates has, it would appear, retreated upon Gordonsville. This place is to the rear of the Rappahannock river, and is connected by rail with Western and Central Virginia, Tennessee, and the southwest. This new position is reported to be much stronger even than that of Manassas, but as the greater portion of their railroad communication has been destroyed by late events in Kentucky and Tennessee, and McClellan is slowly advancing, they may not long be able to hold it.

The following order from the President proves that the movements of the different armies of the Union some weeks ago were all parts of a settled plan:—

EXECUTIVE MANSION, WASHINGTON:
January 27, 1862.

President's General War Order, No. 1.

Ordered,—That the 22nd day of February, 1862, be the day for a general movement of the land and naval forces of the United States against the insurgent forces. That especially

The army at and about Fortress Monroe,
The army of the Potomac,
The army of Western Virginia,
The army near Munfordsville, Kentucky,
The army and flotilla at Cairo,
And a naval force in the Gulf of Mexico,

be ready for a movement on that day.

That all other forces, both land and naval, with their respective commanders, obey existing orders for the time, and be ready to obey additional orders when duly given.

That the Heads of Departments, and especially the Secretaries of War and of the Navy, with all their subordinates, and the General-in-Chief, with all other commanders and subordinates of land and naval forces, will severally be held to their strict and full responsibilities for the prompt execution of this order.

ABRAHAM LINCOLN.

Perhaps the above may be the reason for the sudden evacuation of Manassas by the enemy, and their naval movements in Hampton Roads. Such orders are seldom kept secret, and Davis may have learnt what threatened him, and ordered a retreat in time. It is believed by many qualified to express an opinion on the subject that the enemy's design was to sink all the vessels of war at Hampton Roads, and then to sail up the Chesapeake to Annapolis and Baltimore, with the object of destroying the great fleet of transports now collecting at these two ports. Having thus obtained command of those waters, they would throw a large force upon Newport News, and finally invest Fortress Monroe itself. All this was frustrated by the timely arrival of the little 'Monitor.'

It would be impossible to give you a reasonable idea of the panic produced by the devastations of the iron-clad Confederate battery 'Merrimac.' The forts in New York Harbour and other Northern ports were immediately filled with artillerymen, and it was even proposed to sink stone-laden ships on the New York bar so as to prevent the expected approach of the terrible destroyer. Although she was beaten off the second day by Ericsson's little 'Monitor,' the apprehension is not entirely allayed; fears are entertained by some that the 'Merrimac' is not injured as represented; but inasmuch as she has not shown herself during the week, these surmises may be incorrect. Mr. Fox, the Assistant-Secretary of the Navy, who was present during the second day's action, says she was damaged the previous day by the last broadside of the 'Cumberland;' the 'Monitor' handled her very severely, and the Norfolk papers report her 'only slightly injured,' which is as much as they would be likely to own to. The Secretary states that the 'Merrimac' was coated all over with tallow, and the shot of her antagonist would thus be glanced off without much damage.* She is represented to be armed with eight 10-inch guns, and two 100-pounder Armstrongs. French officers who went on board her at Norfolk Navy-yard report the latter guns to be positively Armstrongs. They are not Whitworths, as will be seen from the following circumstance. When the 'Monitor' and 'Merrimac' were closing in on each other, the former was struck in her turret by one of these rifle projectiles; the bolt penetrated the iron four-and-a-half inches deep, and broke off short, leaving the iron and portions of the lead around immoveably fixed in the tower. The bolt is circular, not hexagonal; and, besides, Whitworth's projectiles are of iron alone.

The captain of Her Majesty's frigate 'Rinaldo,' which arrived a few days since at Fortress Monroe, is stated to have expressed the opinion that nothing could take or hurt the little 'Monitor.' It is very evident that 100-pound rifle shots have scarcely any effect upon her. The only projectiles calculated to damage this new class of vessels are enormously heavier than any yet manufactured in Europe—shot, for instance, fifteen or twenty inches in diameter—spherical, not rifle, because the initial velocity of the former is very much greater than the latter. The naval authorities here are now constructing guns of this calibre on the Rodman principle, the gun in casting being cooled from the centre outwards. Ships like the 'Warrior' and 'La Gloire' will stand a very poor chance against such ordnance as this.

---

* An admirable mode of throwing off shot. The turrets of the 'Monitors' are always coated with it during action, and an American naval commander once informed me that he felt satisfied this 'slushing' was as good a protection as *an additional inch plate of iron.*

The report that barges had been sunk in the channel, so as to prevent the exit of the 'Merrimac,' proves to be a *canard*. Commodore Goldsborough, the flag-officer on that station, has returned from Albemarle Sound, and hoisted his flag on board the 'Minnesota,' a frigate of the same class as the 'Wabash' and our own 'Mersey.' He states his determination to run down the 'Merrimac' under full steam when she next makes her appearance, whether he sink his own ship or not; and as her speed is some eight knots an hour, whilst that of the battery is only five, he may probably make good his design. Several gun-boats have arrived at the scene of action during the present week, and their eleven-inch Dahlgrens will probably render efficient service in the next engagement. These guns throw a solid shot weighing 170lb. The following letter from the chief engineer of the 'Monitor' will prove of interest to the scientific world :—

Iron-clad 'Monitor,' Hampton Roads:
March 9.

My dear Sir,—After a stormy passage, which proved us to be the finest seaboat I was ever in, we fought the 'Merrimac' for more than three hours this afternoon, and sent her back to Norfolk in a sinking condition. Iron-clad against iron-clad. We manœuvred about the bay here, and went at each other with mutual fierceness. I consider that both ships were well fought. We were struck twenty-two times, pilot-house twice, turret nine times, side armour eight times, deck three times. The only vulnerable point was the pilot-house. One of your great logs (9 by 12 inches thick) is broken in two. The shot struck just outside where the captain had his eyes, and it has disabled him, by destroying his left eye, and temporarily blinding the other. The log is not quite in two, but is broken and pressed inward one and a half inches. She tried to run us down and sink us as she did the 'Cumberland' yesterday, but she got the worst of it. Her bow passed over our deck, and our sharp upper edge side cut through the light iron she had upon her stern, and well into her oak. She will not try that again. She gave us a tremendous thump, but did not injure us in the least. We are just able to find the point of contact.

Congress is manfully supporting the President in his emancipationist policy, the advocates of freedom proving themselves largely in the majority. To-day, the Senate has been discussing the bill 'For the release of certain *persons*' (not *chattels*) 'held to service or labour in the District of Columbia.' All slaves are to be emancipated, their owners to present claims for compensation (if loyal citizens) to commissioners appointed by the Secretary of the Treasury. No claim will be allowed for slaves brought into the district after the passing of the Act; and kidnappers of negroes from the district, for the purpose of re-enslaving them, will be punished on conviction with from five to twenty years in the penitentiary. It need not be feared that such an enormous amount of debt will be caused by this scheme of emancipation as the *New York Herald* and other pro-slavery journals represent. Although the offer is made to the Border (not the rebel) States in good faith, few slaveholders will probably accept it, for the Government cannot compensate them for the loss of political power which they have heretofore enjoyed by the three-fifths representation. I speak by book when I state that the endorsement of the President's scheme of emancipation by Congress is mainly intended to give the Government a strong basis of future action. Cost what it may, slavery is doomed; and, however much the national debt may be increased by a general acceptance of the offer, the country will be incalculably richer afterwards.

March 14.

Intelligence has reached this city of a grand concentration of rebel forces in and around Norfolk. Probably some portion of the army lately at Manassas is being directed upon that point; for, if the Confederates lose that position, not merely Virginia, but North Carolina also, is lost to them. The Federal expedition forming at Annapolis is no doubt destined to the Norfolk navy-yard; and, from what I hear, will sail within the next fortnight. Burnside is aware of the evacuation of Manassas, and no fears are expressed for his safety; for should the worst come to the worst, he can soon regain his transports under protection of the gunboats.

Although the matter is kept a profound secret, I believe Commodore Foote's Mississippi expedition has already sailed from Cairo, and is now on its way down the Father of Waters. Island No. 10 is the new stronghold of the rebels; and Beauregard is in command there with a large force, assisted by thirteen gunboats. Island No. 10 is some 120 miles north of Memphis, and is flanked on either side the river by precipitous heights and bluffs. The 13-inch mortar rafts will be tried here for the first time, and, should the island fall, the Mississippi will then be clear to New Orleans. I have heard it flatly stated by men whose opinions are worthy of notice that this city will be in possession of the North within the next two weeks.

No further intelligence from the army up to 3 P.M. to-day. The weather cold and windy, and the roads drying fast.

CHAPTER III.

EMBARKATION OF THE ARMY OF THE POTOMAC FOR THE PENINSULA.

WASHINGTON: March 15.

THE ARMY is rapidly returning to its former position, and as rapidly embarking for some point unknown but to a few. I am unaware whether it be the General's intention to occupy and defend the intrenchments and forts evacuated by the Confederates. I judge not, however, for the chain of batteries round Washington is ample to defend the city, and it is scarcely likely that the enemy will return, having once quitted. There is an immense fleet of light-draught steam transports now lying at Alexandria and the Washington wharves, and troops and stores are being shipped night and day for a southern destination. Rumour will have it that the whole army is going, leaving only sufficient to defend the forts.

'Where are they going?' is a question everybody asks, and some even pretend to know. The *Richmond Examiner* describes as follows the line of defence taken up by the retreated Confederate army, declaring honestly, 'it is assumed now as a necessity in view of the great force which has been collected on the Potomac.' The *Examiner* describes the new line as 'stretching from the Rappahannock River by a grand circle to Cumberland Gap, in the extreme south-western corner of the State, embracing the

Central and the Virginia and Tennessee railroads, the chief cities of Virginia, and the valley of the James, with the canals and railroads within its circumference.' Such being the case, General McClellan will probably seek to land his army in their rear, and several points are selected for the disembarkation of the troops. I do not think the Rappahannock is the point intended, because the country thereabouts is much cut up, and unsuited for the evolutions of large bodies of men; the York River, however, is a broad, deep, and straight stream, and the army might be landed within a day's march of the city of Richmond. Then, again, the James River offers the advantages of a direct approach to the latter capital; but the banks are probably defended by shore batteries, and would require the co-operation of gunboats to effect a landing. Others suggest that the destination of the army is the Nansemund River, so as to co-operate with Burnside and reduce the Norfolk dockyard and the cities in the vicinity; that effected, the army would advance upon Richmond, meeting with but little opposition in its path.

I paid a visit to the Smithsonian Institute last evening, for the purpose of hearing an anti-slavery lecture by Wendell Phillips. The large hall of the institution was crowded by a well-dressed and evidently respectable audience, and on or near the platform were the Vice-President of the Republic, Messrs. Sumner and Wilson, and other members of the United States Senate and House of Representatives. President Lincoln was not present, but Messrs. Nicolay and Hay, his private secretaries, lent a quasi indorsement to the lecturer. Mr. Phillips is a radical Abolitionist of the Garrison school, and until this war advocated the breaking up of the Union as the only means of ridding the country of slavery. Now, however, that under the war power the Constitution means liberty to all, he supports the Government heart and soul, saying he is too much a Yankee not to accept liberty with thirty-four States, when he can get them.

The lecturer commenced by stating he had prepared no discourse, and his speech, though brilliantly eloquent, certainly lacked continuity. He regarded the struggle in Kansas as initiatory of the present contest. He lauded John Brown as having done more towards making liberty the national policy than any man, except William Lloyd Garrison. 'Democracy said to Europe, "I breed heroes; sit you at my feet."' Mr. Phillips appeared to consider that the anti-slavery feeling of the North had forced the President to adopt the views contained in his late special message to Congress; the whole import of that message was an intimation to the Border States as follows: 'Gentlemen, now is your time to sell;' but the lecturer expressed his conviction that the President's suggestions were rather made for the purpose of establishing a future basis of action. The gentlemen on and near the platform showed by their smiles that Mr. Phillips's conclusions were not altogether incorrect. He was unacquainted with rail-splitting, but he understood that a small wedge was first driven into the wood, and larger ones followed after. This message of Mr. Lincoln's was the small wedge, and larger ones are certain to follow. The sentiment was received with laughter and applause by the audience, while those gentlemen who are known to be intimately connected with the Government accepted the position with an approving smile of indorsement. Mr. Phillips regarded the rebellion as a conspiracy to get possession of Washington, for the purpose of ruling the whole country, and it was a great mistake on the part of Jefferson Davis in not taking possession of the city last winter. 'The South came up to the Potomac without men, munitions, or money, but with an idea; and the North came down with men, munitions, and money, but without an idea. Slavery began the war, and the Government had the right out of rebellion to smite slavery to the dust. He thanked God for creating Beauregard, if he did, and every South Carolinian that came up to the Potomac, as they had given the Government the right to destroy slavery. He would send a hundred thousand men into South Carolina, and force the Government into a policy; and when the yellow fever of the South drove out our men, he would garrison the fort with acclimatised negroes, under white officers, and hold them against the world.'

It was strange and most satisfactory to hear a man of Wendell Phillips's antecedents persuading his hearers to support the President; to hear him ejaculate, 'Go on, old man, I am with you.' Times are indeed changed when the straight-out Abolitionists, who have ceaselessly and confessedly endeavoured to break up the Union, can dare to address the public in the city of Washington, and be listened to and applauded by the Vice-President of the United States and the most prominent members of Congress. Old things have indeed passed away when Wendell Phillips, the Cicero of abolition, can league himself with Democrats and Republicans in furtherance of a common policy. There is but one explanation of this seeming enigma. The men of the North know that the reconstruction of the Union, only possible through subjugation of the South, is the certain doom of slavery. Their cause must therefore enlist the sympathies and prayers of all good men throughout the world, and, above all, of liberty-loving Englishmen.

The successes of the 'Merrimac' against wooden ships have awakened the whole country to the importance of iron-plated batteries, and the uselessness of stone defences to harbours and coasts. Little go-ahead Massachusetts, who never lets the grass grow under her feet, has already determined on building two similar vessels to the 'Monitor,' and New York is stirring in the same direction. An equally important move is to be made in reference to the canals running northward to the great lakes. All the locks are to be widened and lengthened, so as to admit the passage of iron batteries through the interior of the country. The Federal Government is seized with unwonted energy. Several of the new and nearly finished sloops-of-war and gunboats are to be iron-plated forthwith, and many of the serviceable frigates are to be razeed and treated in the same manner. Senator Hale, the chairman of the Senate Committee on Naval Affairs, has introduced a bill for the construction of an iron-clad battery of not less than five or six thousand tons burden: the vessel is to be of enormous strength and speed, and capable of acting as a ram. 1,000,000 dollars are set down for the cost of this battery. 13,000,000 dollars additional are proposed to be appropriated for iron-clad gunboats, and half a million more for extending the facilities of the Washington navy-yard, so as to roll and forge plates for armoured ships. 783,000 dollars are also set down for completing the celebrated Stevens submarine iron floating battery, and which has been building at Hoboken, near New York, since 1840. This, the first of iron batteries, is 400 feet long, stronger than anything yet projected in Europe or America, and is calculated for a speed of twenty miles per hour, or seventeen miles when submerged. Those engineers who have been permitted to view the ship, if such it may be termed, assert that never has there been such a concentration of strength and locomotive power in any vessel yet built. The battery would certainly sink any iron-plated ship now afloat. The Emperor Napoleon has the reputation in Europe of having first designed these iron vessels for war purposes; but it is known here that he obtained his ideas from this self-same Stevens battery during his residence in the United States.

I extract the following from the Philadelphia *Ledger*. War preparations evidently, even in America, cannot be carrried on without a large increase of the burdens of the people:—

The public debt of the United States on the 1st of next July, it is estimated, will amount to 750,000,000 dollars. If the rebellion should be crushed by that time, the Government will still require an extraordinary annual expenditure to keep itself in a position to master the spirit of discord which the rebellion has evoked. The interest on the debt already incurred, some of it bearing 7·30 per cent., would amount to about 50,000,000 dollars, with a sinking fund of 10,000,000 dollars. It is believed that the army cannot be reduced with safety to less than 100,000 men, costing 75,000,000 dollars annually. Our coast defences and navy will cost 65,000,000 dollars; the civil list 50,000,000 dollars, making a total of 250,000,000 dollars as the annual expenditure. The total revenue from the old and new tariffs will amount to only 50,000,000 dollars, leaving 200,000,000 dollars to be raised by extraordinary means.

March 17, 1 P.M.

I have just seen a telegram from Cairo, on the Mississippi, stating that Commodore Foote, with his fleet of iron-clad gunboats and 13-inch mortar-rafts, was within two miles of Island No. 10. Contrary to former reports, this island is so far from evacuated, that numerous batteries frown on the assailants, and large bodies of troops flank the approaches on the two banks. Beauregard is understood to be in command of the defenders, and Bishop (General) Polk acts as his lieutenant. The despatch was dated 10.30 P.M. yesterday (Sunday), and the attack was not expected to commence until this morning. Probably you will hear of the fall of the place by telegram to Boston. Our mail for Europe closes here in two hours.

Island No. 10 is situated nearly opposite the town of Obionville, on the left bank of the Mississippi, twelve miles below Hickman, and about one hundred and ten above the city of Memphis. This island in possession of the Union forces, there will probably be little opposition thence to New Orleans, which city is represented to be undefended up to the present time. A confident belief is expressed by parties likely to know, that New Orleans will be occupied by the Federal armies within the next fortnight: General Halleck will follow the gunboats with his forces, and General Butler will enter the city from the Gulf. There are few Confederate troops in that vicinity, and the inhabitants will rather consent to a surrender than submit to a bombardment.

I hear that General Sherman, in command at Port Royal, is superseded by General Hunter, lately acting on the western bank of the Mississippi. Sherman has a horror of responsibility, and is far too cautious and much too dyspeptic.

Major-General Banks is at present in this city, summoned here by General McClellan. I understand that his army (it is ridiculous calling it a mere division) is about to march from Northern Virginia to Centreville. This shows that the Army of the Potomac proper is likely to embark *en masse* for some Southern point—where, we know not as yet. The embarkation of the troops continues in great haste.

I hear it stated that the bill for emancipation in the district of Columbia will receive the President's signature during the present week. The Confiscation Bill (which frees the slaves of rebels, that is to say, all the slaves in the Cotton States and Eastern Virginia) is expected to pass within two weeks. The good work is making rapid headway.

March 20.

An army of 150,000 men is not moved in a day. The embarkation of troops and *matériel* at Alexandria still continues, while many regiments proceed hence to Annapolis, where an immense fleet of transports awaits their arrival. General McClellan has established his headquarters at the former city, and personally superintends the embarkation, everything being conducted with commendable secrecy. The Army of the Potomac has been divided into five *corps d'armée,* commanded by Major-Generals M'Dowell, Heintzelman, Keyes, Sumner, and Banks; and I now learn that three corps will be landed at different points on the eastern shores of Virginia. I am informed that one, at least, will forthwith proceed to Fortress Monroe; and being reinforced there by several regiments now under General Wool, will cross Chesapeake Bay to the mouth of the Nansemund River, and proceed to invest the city and dockyard of Norfolk. The fears lately expressed for the safety of Burnside's army prove to have been unfounded, for the General has turned up victorious at Newbern, on the Neuse River, far away to the southward. The Confederates are known to have concentrated a large force at Suffolk in defence of Norfolk; but, should it be a part of the plan of campaign to effect a junction of his forces with those about to land by the Nansemund, there will be little difficulty, for the transports will bring his little army in quick time through Pamplico and Albemarle Sounds to within a short march of the city. I do not, however, think this will be effected for the present: the possession of Newbern menaces the important city of Beaufort and the still more important railroad junction at Goldsborough. Beaufort, North Carolina, is reached from Newbern by a railroad traversing a swamp; and as supplies can alone be brought to the former by this route, the reduction of the place is merely a question of time. A United States casemated work, Fort Macon, commands the approaches to the city seaward, and under the guns of this fort now rides the Confederate privateer 'Nashville.' We shall probably hear shortly that Beaufort, Macon, and the 'Nashville' have lowered their flags to the energetic Burnside. Should this general, however, have received orders to cut off the railroad communication between Virginia and the Gulf States, we shall receive intelligence of a fierce contest at Goldsborough, where the rebels have lost no time in entrenching themselves and massing some of their best regiments.

Should this movement on Goldsborough be successfully accomplished, the result to the South will be incalculably damaging. Until the advance of the Union forces, commencing with the defeat of Zollicoffer, the Confederates had enjoyed much greater facilities for transporting troops, munitions, and stores than their opponents. The railroads in the Slave States, although nothing like so numerous as in the North, afforded them a speedier way of reaching the Border, and almost supplied the deficiency of other means of transportation. The battles of Mill Spring, Forts Henry and Donelson, cut off their western line of communication with the Gulf, and Burnside will shortly endeavour to effect a similar result with the road passing southwards through the Eastern States. The consequence will be as follows. The Union armies, availing themselves of the ocean and rivers, will land army after army in the rear of the enemy, barring their retreat, and forcing them to accept battle under most disadvantageous terms. In the West this has already been accomplished to a considerable extent, and less than a month will see McClellan advancing upon Richmond, with the main army of the rebels probably entrenched northwards, on the Rappahannock.

Commodore Foote finds the taking of Island No. 10 a much more difficult matter than he supposed, and we now learn that the reported capture of the place was premature. I saw a telegram to-day from the gallant sailor, stating that the batteries rose one above the other on the island, and that he should scarcely be successful in his attack until General Pope and his army of 30,000 Union troops made a movement in the rear of the defenders. He describes the position as much stronger than that of Columbus, but expresses a belief that a certain 'traverse' (nautical for trick or kink) 'would astonish Secesh!' The commodore represents his rifle-gun practice as perfect, the gunboats being armed with rifled 80-pounders, and he speaks highly of the efficiency of the mortar rafts. A 13-inch shell had exploded in the Confederate floating battery, 'putting an end to the concern in short metre.' Our latest account from the scene of conflict informs us that General Pope was still at Madrid, ten miles below the island. He is constructing batteries at that point for the purpose of cutting off the retreat of the enemy and their gunboats, and when these are finished (they may be ere this) he will cross the river and attack the Confederates in their rear.

There does not appear to be any escape for the rebels, and we daily expect to hear that 15,000 more prisoners are on their way north, and Generals Beauregard and Polk about to join Buckner and Tilghman at Fort Warren.

It is difficult to keep the run of the daily-occurring victories of the Union forces. Late intelligence from Port Royal tells us of the energetic Dupont capturing town after town on the Florida coast. You will gather full particulars of these triumphs from the files of American papers, but I wish particularly to draw your attention to the occupation of St. Augustine, where the townspeople themselves hoisted the Union flag. Of course there was an attempt to destroy the place by the rebel army previous to evacuating it, but fear of remaining too long prevented their carrying out their design. The rebels tried a similar action in reference to the city of Newbern, just captured by Burnside, the citizens vainly opposing them; and throughout the wide extent of country now the scene of conflict, this seems to be the policy of their leaders. At one of the towns in Northern Virginia, just entered by the army under General Banks, the retreating rebels fired on the place heedless of the women and children inside. They in no case consult the wishes of the people, either in respect to the cities or the stores of cotton and tobacco; everything is to be burned by order of the Confederate Government, and Europeans, forsooth, are to be bamboozled with the lie that all this is done out of pure patriotism. The Southern papers afford sufficient evidence that the masses of the people are allowed to have no voice in the matter.

March 21.

The report that Mr. Commissioner Yancey had been taken prisoner on board a schooner which was endeavouring to run the blockade appears to be confirmed. This eminent personage and *beau idéal* of the Southern slaveholding gentleman had cropped his hair close and shaved his face clean, clothing himself in the garb of a sailor. It is said that a newspaper reporter detected the commissioner through this disguise.

Mr. Jefferson Davis has issued a proclamation calling out all the militia in his dominions between the ages of sixteen and sixty years, ordering them to report to head-quarters by companies. Volunteering in the South does not seem to answer, or there would be no necessity for such a measure as this; but should he succeed in getting the men it is difficult to tell when he will obtain arms for them. How different is the patriotism of the Free States!—they have given nearly 700,000 men to support their Government, although President Lincoln merely asked for 400,000, and Congress only voted him 500,000. It was evident that volunteering in the North would have gone on to past a million, but the War Department put a check on volunteering months ago. It is reported along the lines by fugitive negroes that a perfect panic exists throughout the South, all business being entirely suspended. And no wonder. There is not a Slave State in which the Union armies have not obtained a foothold, and at the most important strategic points they are in great force. The ablebodied whites are hundreds of miles northward, struggling against the fast-advancing foe, and Cottondom is left nearly defenceless. At Richmond the conspirators are quarrelling amongst themselves, their former supporters, particularly amongst their newspapers, daily attacking the management of the war. It is openly asserted that many of the Confederate leaders and chiefs of the bureaus at Richmond are the spies of Mr. Seward; and when such charges as these are made it is easy to see that the rebellion is going to the bad.

3 o'clock P.M.—There is no further news from the West, the last telegram to head-quarters being dated from Cairo thirty-nine hours ago. I think it is highly probable you will hear of the capture of Island No. 10 before the sailing of the steamer to-morrow, and with it the whole army of defenders. All is quiet elsewhere—a lull before the storm.

FAIRFAX SEMINARY, VIRGINIA : March 28.

I have returned to head-quarters of the First New Jersey Brigade, whence I addressed you several letters six months ago; and, as with others of this army of the Potomac, I find the four regiments composing it greatly improved in appearance, drill, and discipline. The General commanding the brigade, Phillip Kearny, has lately performed an act which reflects as much credit on himself as upon the officers and men under him. Being offered the rank of General of Division, he refused the step unless he could take his brigade with him, and when Major-General Franklin was requested to consent to the exchange of the brigade in question, he positively refused, on the ground that it was the best in his division. When the army moved forward to Manassas some weeks ago, General Kearny was the first to occupy Centreville and Fairfax Court House, and some show of dissatisfaction was evinced by his command, when the order came to march back to their old quarters. Fairfax Seminary is about three miles from Alexandria, where the army is embarking as fast as circumstances will permit; but there are rumours that General M'Dowell's *corps d'armée*, which includes Franklin's division, will not leave until the last. The men, I need not say, are most anxious to be off, and I hazard the prediction that no brigade will render more efficient service than that led by General Kearny. It is composed of first-rate *matériel*, well officered, and is the cleanest I have yet seen in this army.

General McClellan has his residence and head-quarters within a stone's-throw of where I am writing. The embarkation at Alexandria is carried on under his supervision, and pushed forward with all possible rapidity, but not sufficiently so to please the grumblers, who are as numerous, if not more so, than similar persons are with us. People in civil life have no idea of the immense train which must follow an army. Take, for instance, a single brigade of 4,000 infantry. Twenty ambulances, twenty-five large army wagons, and nearly 200 horses, have to be provided for, in addition to ammunition, forage, and provisions. The force moving towards Southern Virginia by the Potomac and Chesapeake rivers, numbers at least 100,000 men, so that if we multiply the above items by 25, we may form some idea of the difficulties attendant upon the movement of an army. Recollecting the time necessary to embark our own troops and those of France at the commencement of the Crimean war, we should make proper allowance for the apparent slowness of the present operations.

It is a curious sight to pass through the vast fleet of transports now arriving, departing, and loading, at the once quiet port of Alexandria, on the Potomac. The river steamboats of New York, Philadelphia, and Boston, have been taken up by the Government, and countless schooners and brigs line the shores of the river, giving the neighbourhood the appearance of our 'Pool.' Rapid snorting little tugs flit about from pier to pier, dragging the barks here and there, or steaming away for the South with a long line of vessels attached to them. Stalls are fitted up for horses on the decks of these sailing craft, whilst the tugs themselves are laden with boxes, barrels, &c. The steamers are those long, white-painted floating-houses, which have become familiar to Englishmen through panoramas of the Mississippi—narrow, sharp hulls, over-hanging decks, immense paddle-boxes, and a two or three-storied edifice running the entire length of the vessel. One of these monsters will easily carry 1,000 men—that is to say, a complete regiment—officers and all. The city itself now presents an exceedingly busy appearance, particularly in the neighbourhood of the river, for the wharves and warehouses are covered and filled with army stores of all sorts. It is not alone at Alexandria that this work is going on; some portion of the troops and *matériel* are shipped from Washington, and far more at Annapolis; but two weeks at the least will be necessary to enable all to embark. You will thus perceive that the army of the Potomac is pushing on to Richmond by the river itself, Fortress Monroe being its first resting-place.

March 29.

There appears to be a dead-lock in the proceedings at Island No. 10, but, strange to say, the public as yet evince no impatience. A balloon reconnaissance has been made of the enemy's works, and the fact thereby substantiated, that Commodore Foote's shells mostly exploded beyond the Confederate batteries. The elevation has therefore been depressed, and it is confidently expected that the works will soon be rendered untenable. Commodore Foote has experienced much difficulty from the rapid current of the Mississippi, and the fact that his boats are intended to fight with their bows up stream, instead of down. The vessels are only iron-plated over their bows, and were they laid broadside on the enemy they would probably be sunk by the heavy ordnance of the rebels. I think, however, there may be an intentional delay in the proceedings, more especially as Footé has expressed his belief that the works cannot be reduced until the army attacks the rear of the defenders. General Pope, at New Madrid, on the opposite bank of the river, cannot pass the stream in its present swollen condition, but he effectually bars the retreat of the Confederate gunboats and transports. General Ulysses Grant, the victor of Fort Donelson, is now at Savannah, on the Tennessee River, some ninety miles in a south-easterly direction from Island No. 10. Eighteen miles from Savannah is the town of Corinth, in the northern angle of the State of Mississippi, and here General Beauregard is assembling a large army for the defence of the Mississippi Valley. Generals Polk and Cheatham, according to last accounts, have just joined him; and, if we can believe the Southern papers, Beauregard is now at the head of 80,000 men. We hear, too, that the Confederates have changed their plan of campaign, and that henceforward, instead of weakening themselves by defending numerous points, they will mass their forces and hazard their future on the chances of great battles. The only objection to this lies in the fact of their being much outnumbered by their antagonists, besides which the Western troops under Grant are flushed with a long series of victories, while the Southerners are more or less demoralised. We are daily expecting to hear news of a collision between the two armies, and should Beauregard be defeated, Island No. 10 must immediately be evacuated, since Grant would be able to march westward towards Memphis, cutting off four lines of railroad on his passage

Beauregard's position at Corinth is of the highest strategic importance, the town being at the point of intersection of the Memphis and Charleston railroad and the Mobile and Ohio line. Its possession by the Federal army would thus destroy railroad communication between Tennessee and the Atlantic and Gulf States, cutting off the Confederates from all supplies. The occupation of Corinth by the Union army is so necessary to its final success that we shall probably hear of General Halleck assuming command in person at the expected battle. It was rumoured that Jefferson Davis was about to proceed west for the purpose of taking the chief command at this most important point: but the threatening aspect of affairs in Virginia, and the precarious condition of Norfolk and Richmond, will probably induce him to postpone the trip.

I called this morning upon General McClellan, and found the officers of his staff preparing to leave during the day for Alexandria. The general not being visible at so early an hour, I stepped into a tent pointed me by the sentry, and was immediately interrogated by a young aide-de-camp as to the object of my visit. This officer, apparently some two or three-and-twenty years old, was dressed in the plain dark blue suit of a captain, the unpretending shoulder-straps with two gold lace bars showing his rank. Tall and well-formed, his handsome face was bedecked with moustache and nascent beard, growing *à l'Americaine*; his tent, though roomy, was perfectly Spartan in adornment, being somewhat below the average of most of the volunteer officers. The narrow bed, about two feet six wide, was covered with coarse army blankets, but no sheets, and the entire arrangements betokened a supreme contempt for luxury. He sat on his bed and conversed with me for half an hour, the subject being the conduct of the war and the attitude of the English Government during the present troubles of the great Republic. The young captain's accent was slightly foreign; otherwise his knowledge of our language was perfect, much more than is generally found amongst foreigners. I may as well state that I was conversing with the Count of Paris—a fact of which I was at first unaware, but learned it subsequently by 'guessing,' as they say here. The Count is a powerful young fellow, physically, and I am sure must be a very agreeable companion with his comrades, for his observations to me were both just and witty, and not in the slightest degree tinctured with arrogance. Whatever fortunes may be in store for him, I believe he will prove worthy of them; and he certainly shows himself perfectly at home amongst the Republicans of the New World.

WASHINGTON: March 31. (3. P.M.)

I have come over from the camp to the capital, expecting to find telegraphic and other news, but with little result for my pains. There is, in fact, a considerable dearth of intelligence, both sides in this great struggle being engaged in remarshalling their forces for a supreme effort. The latest news at this moment (the mail closing for Europe in half an hour) is mostly negative. Nothing further from Island No. 10, and affairs unsensational at Fortress Monroe. We have been expecting a new exodus of the terrible 'Merrimac' and her iron-plated consorts, the 'Yorktown' and 'Jamestown;' but it is evident that the first was so mauled by the little giant 'Monitor,' that she has been docked for repairs. Captain Fox, the energetic Assistant Secretary of the Navy, says every preparation has been made to meet her; and his quiet self-possessed manner satisfies me that she will be worse handled on her next exit than heretofore.

General McClellan has taken up his quarters on board one of the New York river-boats, the 'Commodore,' but I think he will not depart until the end of this week. At Fortress Monroe there are now the two *corps d'armée* of Generals Heintzelman and Keyes, representing about 70,000 men, and I hear that General M'Dowell's *corps* will leave this week, which will make 40,000 more. I believe the latter is to land at the mouth of the York River, the best and shortest route to Richmond. Sumner's *corps d'armée* is now in and around Manassas, and that under Banks is advancing upon the same point by the valley of the Shenandoah, but I have no idea or information what their future movements will be. I shall probably leave for the South with the force under General M'Dowell.

CHAPTER IV.

ADVANCE OF GENERAL M'DOWELL'S CORPS UPON WARRINGTON JUNCTION.

BRISCOE'S STATION, ORANGE AND ALEXANDRIA
RAILROAD, VIRGINIA: April 5.

BRIGADIER-GENERAL KEARNY'S command, composed of the 1st, 2nd, 3rd, and 4th New Jersey Regiments, left their winter quarters at Alexandria Seminary this morning, and embarked on the railroad cars about one mile from the latter place. This brigade is the first of General Franklin's division of 16,000 men; and the whole of Major-General M'Dowell's *corps d'armée*, of which it forms a part, is under orders to follow it along the line of railroad to the banks of the Rappahannock. An order was issued yesterday morning by the Secretary of War, constituting two new military departments, M'Dowell being placed at the head of the department of the Rappahannock, extending from the east of the Potomac River to the Blue Ridge Mountains, and General Banks commanding in that of the Shenandoah, west of the Blue Ridge and east of the Alleghanies. M'Dowell's *corps d'armée* consists of four divisions, and is now said to number between 60,000 and 70,000 men and ninety pieces of artillery. Such is the report of men who ought to be acquainted with the true state of the case, but your readers can take it *cum grano salis*. The department of the Rappahannock extends south to the city of Richmond, and the troops are in high spirits at the prospect of an early brush with the main army of the rebels under Joe Johnston, who is said to be entrenching himself between the Rappahannock and Rapidan rivers.

We left the Seminary about eleven o'clock. The morning was wet and cheerless, and as we all expected to be off soon after *réveillée*, and the tents had been struck at an early hour and packed in the wagons, we were nearly wet through before starting. Twenty minutes' walk through mud ankle-deep brought us to the railroad, where we found four long trains awaiting our arrival, and General Franklin already on the ground to superintend the embarkation. The railroad at this point runs through a valley, and it was a cheering sight to watch 4,000 men descending from the hills at a quick step to the music of their bands, and giving volley after volley of cheers to the General of Division. The troops were packed closely in the cars or carriages, as we call them, and huddled together on the roofs, until there was imminent danger of the latter being crushed in; indeed, it was found necessary, during the journey, to support the roofs with poles, the pioneers proving themselves particularly handy in the emergency. We understood that our destination was Warrington Junction, eight or ten miles beyond Manassas, but the road was in so dilapidated a condition, the trains so heavy, and the grades so trying, that we alighted at nightfall at Briscoe's, and are now encamped about four miles beyond the celebrated field of Bull Run. Several times during the trip we found the grades too steep for our engine, and at last half our cars were disconnected, and one portion of the train was hurried forward to the nearest switch or siding (nearly all the railroads in the South are single tracks),

when the locomotive returned to fetch the remainder.
Another time we waited for the second train to come up
and push us over the hill, and we had leisure to examine
a deserted rebel encampment, or town of well-constructed
log huts, as it should rather be called. We found nearly
the entire of the ground in and around this encampment
covered with graves, the Confederate officers having permitted the burials to be made within half a dozen yards of
the huts. Judging by the coarse inscriptions on the head-
stones, most of the interments belonged to Alabama
regiments, with a slight sprinkling of Texans, and the
mortality must have been enormous.

CATLETT'S STATION, NEAR WARRINGTON:
April 6.

A bright warm sunrise this morning gave us the hope
of an early spring, but the weather is so changeable in this
State of Virginia, that we can count only on a single day
of fine weather. Early hours are the rule in camps, and
when we got from under the blankets, at six o'clock, the
men detailed as cooks had already prepared the modest
breakfast for the troops, and the smoke of a hundred fires
rose spirally towards the heavens. The four regiments
composing General Kearny's brigade were encamped on
four hills lying parallel to each other, and had it not been
for the pine forests, bounding the prospect, and the numerous brooks coursing down the slopes, we might have
thought ourselves in the South Downs of England. General Kearny possesses the proper military horror of wagon
trains, and the baggage of officers and men alike had been
reduced to the minimum; the former were permitted to
carry small wall tents, but the latter sheltered themselves
beneath the uncomfortable *tentes d'abri*, which afford

almost as much protection from the weather as a medium-sized pocket-handkerchief. The *impedimenta* carried by a private in this army are as follows:—A knapsack averaging 30 lbs., a thick woollen blanket, a tin canteen holding three pints, five days' rations, forty rounds of ammunition, and half one of the above shelter tents. The musket is either our long Enfield or the Springfield rifle, weighing about the same, but a few of the regiments are armed with the 'Minié' or the 'Belgian;' here and there we find some of the old smooth-bore, but these are being rapidly exchanged for the improved weapon.

The First New Jersey Brigade is the first brigade in the first division of Major-General M'Dowell's *corps d'armée*, which, until the day before yesterday, was the first corps in the army of the Potomac. I am marching with the first regiment of the brigade, and am in front of the advance; but we hear that many Federal troops are before us—General Blencker's division among the rest. Probably these forces are merely occupying the Confederate position at Manassas and the approaches towards the Rappahannock, to be vacated by them when M'Dowell's *corps d'armée* has advanced from its winter quarters.

I breakfasted this morning at the house of a farmer near our camp. He of course pretended to be an 'Union man,' and opposed to the heresy of Secession; but little confidence can be placed in the loyalty of any of the inhabitants of States where slavery exists by law. The Border Slave States are allied by pride to those of the Gulf, and will do anything in their power to assist them, if they get the opportunity. When the Union armies approach, the people are either silent and morose, or out of the way; and this is more emphatically the case where Virginia is concerned. The policy of the Federal Government, let it be called by what name it may, is really *coercion* towards the Border States, and *subjugation* towards those of the Gulf; and if the people of the former appear to welcome the Northern armies it is only because they fear to evince their real feelings. And so must it be so long as anything remains— in fact, or hope—of the political power of slavery. The farmer at whose house I took breakfast appeared to be a quiet, harmless individual, and seemingly indifferent to politics; he explained that the Southern troops had carried off his stock, destroyed his fences, &c., and he also spoke on the excessive prices of provisions and clothing since the commencement of the war.

The brigade started from Briscoe's Station at noon, marching along the railroad towards Catlett's, distant about seven miles The Orange and Alexandria road is almost entirely owned by Northern capitalists, and none but white labour, mostly Irish, has been engaged upon it. For these reasons the Southerners always regard it as an Abolitionist line, and I hear that long before the present troubles the directors had to keep guards constantly at their bridges to prevent their being destroyed. The road runs through a very hilly country, and the curves are numerous and sharp, and the grades exceedingly heavy; it is said that the engineer who built the line received so much extra for every curve, so as to avoid the expense of viaducts. The sleepers are miserably poor, nothing but raw pine logs of no great weight; it is a wonder that the trains do not more frequently run off the track. There must have been an immense business carried on upon this road during the past twelve months, judging by the dilapidated condition of the rails and sleepers; the former are worn away on the outer edge, and very unsafe, and the sleepers are not merely rotten and worm-eaten, but the ballasting between them is gone, obliging the troops to step, or rather jump, from one to the next. Seven miles of such marching was by no means pleasant even to those who did not carry a musket and knapsack. A mile or two from Briscoe's we got into a more level country, and the scenery became very beautiful. I have never yet seen any land which appeared so adapted for wheat as this State of Virginia; and the troops seemed to have the same opinion, for they amused themselves during the march with selecting farms and telling each other what produce they would raise 'after the war was over.' The country undulates gradually, and here and there are level plains between the hills, intersected in all directions by clear running streams. What a magnificent State Virginia would be were she consecrated to free labour! As it is, the State is not half cleared of its woods, the richest lands are undrained, and the countless brooks course down the hills to the many rivers—useless because neglected. Virginia might supply half Europe with wheat were she settled by men from the Free States; but there is no hope for her so long as she remains under the curse of slavery.

In the Southern States you look vainly for anything having the appearance of a village: now and then you come upon a house or two, but the distances between them are so remote that your first emotion is one of surprise. As the troops marched along the line, we came upon a farmer-looking individual who gave us the only God-speed with which we have yet been favoured: he looked at us with a smiling face, and said, 'Go it, boys; I'm glad to see so many of you.' Such words in such a place naturally astonished us, and a dozen voices from the ranks immediately asked him what State he was from, when he informed us he was born in New Jersey, but had been settled some years in Virginia.

Farther on we overtook a Virginian gentleman out with his dogs for a stroll; but he, of course, had no word of consolation or look of approval for the invaders of Southern rights. These were all the people we met during our walk of seven miles, and this walk may be taken as a fair sample of what a traveller meets in the Southern country. As we neared the termination of the day's march the evidences became more frequent of the desolation caused by the retreating Confederates. The bridges on the railroad were all destroyed, the rails carried off, and the sleepers burnt, the object of course being to retard the pursuing army. This work of destruction was evidently performed in a leisurely and thorough manner. The bridges, being all of wood, were burned; and the stone abutments in many cases blown away by gunpowder; but, notwithstanding all the ruin, the advancing armies will not long be retarded. Several of the bridges have already been built anew, and I am informed that during the present week the line will be completed from Washington to the banks of the Rappahannock River. The measurements have been taken all along the road, and the bridges are being rapidly constructed at the capital, and, when finished, they will be forwarded by trains to their various destinations. I understand that the structure over the Rappahannock was no less than 1,200 feet in length, but this has gone the same as the rest. At Catlett's Station, and away to the latter point, the rails are quite useless: the sleepers have been taken from the road and piled up at equal distances, the rails laid on top, and fire applied to the heap; nothing now remains of eight or ten miles of road but black ashes and warped and twisted rails. The apparatus for supplying water to the locomotives have all disappeared, the locomotives and cars have been carried away South, and nothing in fine remains but the graded road. Nevertheless, a few weeks will put the line in far better condition than it has been in for years.

It will of course be asked, Does the South intend continuing this terrible work of destruction wherever and whenever the Northern armies enter its confines? If these railroads and public works are to be destroyed, and these towns and cities burned up, what is to become of the mass of the Southern people? Surely the millions of Southerners can have no part in this widespread devastation.

WARRINGTON JUNCTION:
April 7.

Finding that the New Jersey Brigade would remain at Catlett's Station during this day, and hearing that the 12th Massachusetts regiment was on the other side of the river called Cedar Run, I took a walk of two miles this morning in advance of General Kearny's troops, intending to return during the afternoon. But, alas! it has suddenly come on to rain in torrents, and I am compelled to remain here for the night. Cedar Run is the main branch of the Occoquan river, which empties itself into the Potomac some thirty-five miles below the city of Alexandria; Bull Run, on which was fought the famous battle last July, is the northern fork of the stream. Both branches take their rise in the Blue Ridge Mountains, which are plainly distinguishable here at a distance of forty miles.

The 12th Massachusetts regiment forms part of General Abercrombie's brigade, and belongs to the fifth *corps d'armée* of the army of the Potomac, commanded by General Banks. I cannot learn how it is that this brigade is now stationed at this point, for the late order of the

Secretary of War confines the force under Banks to the Department of the Shenandoah, on the other side of the Blue Ridge. Maybe the regiments composing it are merely here until the arrival of M'Dowell's corps, but none of the officers nor General Abercrombie himself can give any explanation. Their orders are simply to remain here until further notice, and that is sufficient for soldiers. Banks himself is with the advance of his command, at Woodstock, whither he has followed the defeated army of Jackson, and it is supposed he will continue to march forward into Southern Virginia, while M'Dowell progresses in the same direction on this side of the Blue Ridge. Fremont's command commences at the eastern confines of Banks's Department, that is to say, west of the Alleghanies, and he too is advancing southwards. Nobody seems to form any opinions as to the strength of the force under Major-General Fremont, but it is now being largely increased by the addition of the brigades under Acting Major-General Blencker. I learn to-day that the division has lately been detached from the Department of the Potomac, and is now on its way for Staunton, but nothing of this was known when I left Washington except in official circles. All these movements seem to point to a simultaneous parallel advance of the three armies under M'Dowell, Banks, and Fremont, towards Southern Virginia, while McClellan, with his three *corps d'armée*, hems in the rebels at Richmond from the other direction. I do not think it over-stating the numbers of these different commands at 300,000 men.

I called upon General Abercrombie, whom I found quartered at a miserable little cottage, about a mile from the river. He told me that the 'contrabands'—in other words, the negroes—were coming to him in such numbers as to be a serious cause of anxiety, and he expressed his fears that the farther the Union armies advanced into the Slave States, the more difficult the question would become. He is right in this, for the Government must deal with the issue on the spur of the moment, and not on political grounds alone. The rebel troops clear off everything in the shape of provisions as they retire, and the runaway slaves seek from the Northern commanders not so much liberty as the very necessities of life. While Congress is debating the question of emancipation, and philanthropists are arguing whether to employ the negroes or to transport them *nolens volens* to remote colonies, the Commissary Department of the United States army suddenly finds itself charged with an enormous and ever-increasing incubus, which never entered into its calculations. The Union forces have scarcely entered the enemy's country as yet, but already the demand for rations more than frightens the Federal officers. What will it be when the Northern armies penetrate beyond the Border States, and enter those districts where the blacks increase at a far greater ratio than their white masters?

April 9.

I am still at the camp of the 12th Massachusetts, blocked in by an impassable ocean of mud. Since the day before yesterday, when I quitted Catlett's Station, it has 'stormed' incessantly, rendering it physically impossible for me to return, owing to the rise in the numerous streams. A little rivulet, which I stepped across on Monday, had become so swollen yesterday morning that horses could with difficulty get through it; and if this be the case with a nameless brook, what must it be with the rivers? We are half swallowed up in mud, or rather slush, and visits from tent to tent have now become few and far between, for the 'sacred soil' rises above the ankles and almost sucks off one's boots. During the past sixty hours it has rained, hailed, mizzled, and snowed, and the whole country at the present writing is covered with the dreary mantle of winter. The scouts drop in now and then, worn out with hunger and exposure, and I have just learned that there are no rations for the brigade, owing to the non-arrival of the supply train. Colonel Webster* tells me that throughout this section of the country the land is literally covered with springs, lying only a short distance below the surface, and that even on the hills water can always be obtained at a depth of only a foot or two. The camping ground of this regiment is on a considerable elevation, and yet we might be at the bottom of a valley, judging by the mud around us.

April 10.

I managed to effect my return to the New Jersey Brigade this morning, in company with Colonel Webster and Lieutenant-Colonel Bryan. We rode here on horseback, but it was about as much as the animals could do to pull through the mud and swim the torrent of Cedar Run.

The first train from Washington in three days arrived here this afternoon, bringing us intelligence of a great victory in Tennessee over the combined forces of Beauregard, Polk, Breckinridge, and Bragg, and the equally welcome news of the capture of Island No. 10. These events may change the present plan of campaign, and orders are anxiously looked for by the men and officers of

---

* Son of the great statesman, Daniel Webster. The Colonel was killed at the second battle of Bull Run, fought August 30, 1862. His body was found on the field, the corpse stripped naked to the skin.

this brigade. No train has left here for Washington since our arrival, the railroad to Catlett's Station having only just been completed; but I am in hopes of despatching this letter in time for the mail of Saturday.

April 11.

Generals M'Dowell and Franklin have just arrived here with orders for the whole of this division to return immediately to Alexandria, there to be shipped to Fortress Monroe. The troops receive the news with acclamation, but Major-General M'Dowell, if we may judge by his countenance, does not appear to relish the change in the programme. The Department of the Rappahannock, created a week ago, is apparently knocked on the head. The impression seems to be that the late victories in the West, by opening up the road to New Orleans, have compelled the evacuation of Virginia by the Confederates, who are now endeavouring to withdraw their armies from the Border States into the cotton region.

April 13.

After a long and tedious march of upwards of forty miles, we arrived at Alexandria this morning, and are in hourly expectation of being ordered to embark for Southern Virginia. The offing is full of transports, amongst them the immense Pacific mail steamer 'Constitution,' which is capable of taking away an entire brigade. General Franklin's division will sail immediately, and camp rumours are to the effect that we shall land above Yorktown, so as to take the enemy in the rear. You will perceive that the campaign is now commencing in good earnest, and my letters will in consequence be much more interesting than heretofore.

CHAPTER V.

AMERICAN IRON-CLADS.

WASHINGTON: April 15.

THE contest between the iron-plated batteries 'Merrimac' (called by the Confederates the 'Virginia') and the little 'Monitor' (*alias* the 'Ericsson'), appears to have wakened you up in Europe. It will, therefore, be both instructive and interesting to learn what Americans are doing in regard to this new phase in naval construction. I do not pretend to any acquaintance with the movements of the Confederates further than what may be gathered from such questionable authorities as the Southern journals, and I doubt whether science will be much the loser from the prevailing ignorance on that subject. The mechanical skill of the Slave States has never been remarkable: the manufacture of iron within their confines is of comparatively recent date; and they are necessarily controlled in their efforts by the want of many articles. True, we hear rumours of numerous floating batteries in process of completion, at New Orleans, Mobile, Savannah, Charleston, &c., and we learn, also, that the construction is 'turtle-formed' in all instances; but we possess no reliable information on any other battery than the now-famous 'Merrimac.' It must be borne in mind, too, that the latter is simply a 'make-shift,' a floating fort of iron built upon the lower part of the hull of a heavy frigate—the idea being taken from the sloping railroad-iron bomb-proof used against Fort Sumter. The idea is apparently a good one as against wooden ships; but it remains to be seen whether the 'Merrimac' can hold her ground in contests with such batteries as are now being constructed in the Northern States. There are two other iron-plated vessels at Norfolk—the 'Yorktown' and 'Jamestown;' but these are scarcely worth more than passing notice, being slightly-built river boats, and obviously unfit to carry heavy armour-plates. We have as yet no knowledge whatever of a Confederate iron floating battery, ship or ram, which is more than an adaptation of an old vessel.

What the Northern States are doing is most important to us to learn, now that we are about plunging ourselves still deeper into the quicksand of expenditure. If we must have iron fleets, it may be advisable to take other models than the 'Warrior' and 'La Gloire,' and to arm them with heavier ordnance than one, two, or three hundred pounders. The United States are reforming their naval affairs in everything pertaining to this subject, and I design to give you some of their experience based on experiments of the past six months. The improvements have reference to the following particulars:—

      1. Form of hull.
      2. Description of plates.
      3. Motive power.
      4. Armament.

No particular form of hull has been decided upon as most effective, and numerous batteries are being constructed differing materially from each other. Ericsson's successful experiment with the 'Monitor' has naturally enlisted most people in favour of his plan, and he has been awarded contracts for six others on that principle. One of them, now in course of construction, will be upwards of 300 feet in length, and covered with 8-inch thick plates, only 18 inches of the hull appearing above the water. The walls of the revolving turret, 26 feet in diameter, will be 18 inches thick, and the armament two 20-inch solid shot guns. The 'Warrior' or 'Black Prince' would fare no better against this vessel than the 'Cumberland' and 'Congress' against the 'Merrimac.' Another form of battery is that of the 'Galena,' which will sail from New York to Norfolk during the present week. The 'Galena' was built at Mystic, Connecticut, and three or four others of similar construction are now nearing completion at Philadelphia and elsewhere. Her length is 200 feet, width 36 feet, draft of water $11\frac{1}{2}$ feet, and burden 738 tons. Above the water-line her sides slope inwards at an angle of forty-five degrees, and she is completely iron-plated, bows, stern, sides, and deck, the weight of the armour being 400 tons. She is pierced for six heavy guns, throwing solid round shot or elongated projectiles. The port-holes are raised and lowered by means of levers, and her sides are perfectly smooth the bolt-heads not being visible. The speed of the 'Galena' is calculated at twelve knots, and she is intended for sea-voyages, not, as in the case of the 'Monitor,' for harbour defence alone. I have described in a previous letter the plan of the immense 'Stevens' Battery;' there are still other batteries now in progress, modelled after the 'Merrimac,' but these will not be completed for some time to come. Amongst them is the 50-gun frigate 'Roanoke,' sister ship to the 'Merrimac.'

There has been a vast amount of experiment on iron plates, both by the Government and private individuals, single plates being viewed with distrust. There are shields composed of layers of iron, with packings of timber and caulking between, and plates of thick corrugated iron, bolted upon beams, with several inches of oakum intervening. I have seen at the Navy Department a number of damaged plates taken off the gunboats of Foote's squadron, after the bombardment of Forts Donelson and Henry; the solid shields, of three and four inches thick, were split by the enemy's shot, whilst those composed of successive layers were merely indented. One of the former was struck by a projectile at an angle of about thirty degrees, the iron splitting in the region of the first point of contact, and the shot flying off at an angle of about twenty degrees. Beyond being indented, the thin plates were not damaged.

The favourite mode of propulsion is by two screws, one on each side of the rudder. This enables the vessel to turn completely round within her own length, and it also gives a vast increase of speed and independence of the steering apparatus, should the latter become damaged. The speed of the batteries, as a general thing, will be in the neighbourhood of fifteen miles the hour—of course, not including those nearing completion. There is another principle which does not seem to have attracted the attention of European constructors—namely, the power of submersion.

The contest with the sloping-sided 'Merrimac' has set the gun-founders here on the *qui vive*, and Dahlgren, Parrott, and Rodman are now casting guns of vastly greater calibre than anything yet talked of in Europe. American artillerists, like the French, do not believe in breech-loaders, but all their guns are remarkable for a great thickness of metal at the breech, and, so far as I know, not one of them has ever burst. Rodman's principle is peculiarly adapted for heavy cannon, such as 15in. and 20in. bore. The vast body of metal is cooled by streams of water introduced in a certain manner into the casting, and the gun is thus cooled gradually from the interior towards the outer surface. The 15-in. 'Union' and 'Lincoln' guns at Fortress Monroe are cast on the above principle. The form of projectile has attracted much attention from scores of inventors, the object being to rip open the sloping sides of vessels like the 'Merrimac.' Round shot glance off, and conical very seldom strike as designed, especially at long ranges. I have seen a specimen of a number sent to Fortress Monroe, which are intended to 'gouge' the enemy's plates; they are six inches in diameter and fifteen inches long. At a distance of about two-thirds from the base the shot assumes the form of the neck and shoulder of a bottle; the end is made of steel, perfectly flat, the edges sharp, and its diameter three inches. The other day I was shown a conical musket-ball of glass, which had been fired through a thin iron plate without any damage to itself; may-be we shall eventually discover a better substance than iron for projectiles against plates of that material.

The statement has lately been made by a member of our Government that by the close of the present year we shall have ten iron-plated ships afloat. By the same period the United States will have forty! I have been favoured with particulars of the following vessels, and you will perceive how much more effective are the American batteries than our unwieldy Warriors, and how much less costly, too. It must be borne in mind that three requisites are looked for in these new ships—invulnerability, weight of metal, and speed. The 'Warrior' and 'Black

Prince,' if I remember rightly, are partially plated with 4-inch iron: the batteries constructing here are double that thickness. The ordnance on the English ships might hammer away all day on vessels like the 'Monitor' and 'Stevens' Battery' with no more effect than the firing of the ' Cumberland ' and ' Congress ' on the 'Merrimac;' while one or two shots at close quarters from the former would sink the ' Warrior ' to Davy's locker. The six-turreted battery which we are about constructing is to be armed with 68-pounders—what effect would these have against eighteen inches thick of iron of the American turret, or the eight-inch-thick iron of the submerged deck ? Thirty 68-pounders—in other words, the broadside of a sixty-gun ship—would only throw the same amount of metal as the two twenty-inch guns of the American vessel. The comparison does not end here. It is obvious that as we diminish the number of guns, we increase the speed of the battery, inasmuch as greater room is given for the engines. The naval authorities of the United States have recognised this truth, and the floating batteries intended for sea-voyages will not carry over fifty men. They will not require more either to work the ship or the guns.

The 'Monitor,' now at Fortress Monroe, cost only 275,000 dollars, or, in English currency, about £57,000. She is 766 tons burden, her displacement 1,038 tons, and her draught of water 10 feet; she is armed with two 11-inch guns.

The 'Galena' is now getting her armament on board, and will sail for the fortress this week. Her burden is 738 tons; displacement, 1,294 tons ; draft, 11 7-12 feet; and cost, 235,250 dollars. She carries two rifled 100-pounders and four 9-inch guns.

The 'Stevens' Battery,' commenced twenty years ago at Hoboken, opposite New York city, is 3,500 tons burden, and her draft 19 feet. The cost of this immense vessel, carrying five 15-inch smooth-bore Columbiads and two 10-inch rifled guns, will only be 1,283,000 dollars (about £270,000). These guns command every point of the compass, and her broadside will therefore be 3,000 lbs. Are the sides of the 'Warrior,' 'Black Prince,' or 'La Gloire,' strong enough to resist the shock of a ton and a half of metal? Would it not also be advisable for English taxpayers to compare the cost and weight of the 'Warrior's' broadside with those of the 'Stevens' Battery,'—in other words, the cost of the two ships themselves?

The 'Ironsides,' now completing at Philadelphia, and to be ready for sea in three months, is 3,486 tons burden; displacement, 3,699 tons; draft, 13 feet; and the contract price, 780,000 dollars. She will carry two rifled 200-pounders, and sixteen 11-inch guns.

Six 'Ericsson Batteries' are now in course of construction under the supervision of Ericsson himself, and will be in commission by the end of the year. Their burden will be 1,085 tons; displacement, 1,450 tons; draft, 11 feet; cost, 400,000 dollars each; and their armament, two 15-inch guns. The little 'Monitor' proved herself sea-worthy except in one particular, namely, the ventilators on deck, which being only 4 feet high, allowed the water to wash in. All future vessels on this principle will be ventilated through the roof of the revolving turret. It must not be imagined from the late refusal of the 'Monitor' to engage the 'Merrimac,' that her officers were fearful of the result; the reasons of the declension were as follow:—The Government knew that the object of the enemy in coming out was to make a passage to Yorktown for their iron-plated ships, the 'Jamestown' and 'Yorktown'—and the 'Monitor' in remaining at anchor effectually barred the channel between the shoals. Had the 'Galena' been there, the challenge of the 'Merrimac' would have been accepted; but it was useless to needlessly imperil the safety of the ships of war and transports by permitting the 'Monitor' to engage her single-handed. The 'Merrimac,' since her contest a month ago, has been fitted with a long prow, designed to crush in the thin iron plates of her formidable antagonist beneath her strong upper works; and I hear also that the Confederates had prepared a trap for her, had she ventured to follow the 'Merrimac' into the Elizabeth river. Heavy piles were driven across the channel, leaving an entrance of only 100 feet; an old United States ship of the line, the 'Germantown,' lay moored within this enclosure, and when the 'Monitor' should pass the entrance the ship was to be swung round so as to bar her exit. You will perceive that the Government is admirably well informed as to the doings of the rebels.

Numbers of these iron batteries, many of them with revolving turrets, are being constructed in the interior of the country, some being specially designed for operations in the Western rivers. By improvements in the interior water communication, deepening channels, widening locks of canals, &c., it will be possible to concentrate most of these vessels on any required point from the great lakes to the Gulf of Mexico. Under two Congressional appropriations, 23,000,000 of dollars are devoted to the construction of these batteries, and Congress will shortly add to this sum 7,000,000 dollars additional, lately voted for improvements in fortifications. The debate in the House of

Commons has silenced most of the opposition to this proposal.

I would remark in conclusion, that the principle of the batteries now being constructed under the auspices of the United States Government is the raft, a slightly arched deck being placed on a comparatively narrow hull. A raft offers but little resistance to the waves, and these vessels ought therefore to be good sea-boats; whilst, at the same time, much less surface is exposed to the enemy's shot than in the old-fashioned ships of the 'Warrior' build.

I cannot close my remarks on this important topic without acknowledging the obligations I am under to officers of the United States Government for the above information. You will agree with me that their course can alone be dictated by the desire to maintain friendly relations with a people whose rulers have not always shown themselves careful to act in a similar spirit. Will it not be sound policy for our Government to seek to cultivate the most friendly relations with a power whose army numbers 600,000 men, and whose iron fleet will shortly surpass the combined squadrons of the two most powerful nations in Europe? It is false and stupid to suppose that because the aims and interests of the English and American people are similar, they must therefore be antagonistic; and the day, we may hope, is not far distant when the two branches of the Anglo-Saxon race will unite upon a common policy, not more for their own advantage than for the benefit of the whole human race.*

* There is much ignorance in reference to the American 'Monitors' on both sides the Atlantic, some people extravagantly overrating their merits, others improperly depreciating them. This class of vessels was not designed for the ocean at all, but for harbour and coast service against other iron-

CHAPTER VI.

A GENERAL VIEW OF AFFAIRS.

April 16.

THE reinforcing of General McClellan is confined to the division of General Franklin. General M'Dowell still retains his department of the Rappahannock, and his *corps d'armée*, now consisting of three divisions, is concentrating itself on the banks of Cedar Run, at Catlett's station. An immense pontoon train was sent forward a day or two back, from which it may be inferred that M'Dowell will cross the Rappahannock before long; but as both the scouts and the runaway negroes report that few rebel troops remain between that river and the Rapidan, we need scarcely look for active operations in Central Virginia for some time to come. The major part of the Confederate army is now defending the lines covering Yorktown, and, if rumour be correct, the enemy at that point numbers some

clads. Speed is not a requisite in their construction, for they are intended to keep in shoal water where sea-going ships cannot get at them. They carry but two or four guns of enormous calibre: one of their projectiles, if properly landed, would tear a hole in the side of the 'Warrior' or 'La Gloire' which would sink or disable her. The Monitors have been used in siege operations during this war on account of the absence of other vessels; but when the sea-going ironclads now in course of construction by the United States are completed, the Monitors will be kept solely for harbour defence. No ship built for ocean service can hope to contend successfully against two or more of these turreted craft in harbour or on the coast.

100,000 men. We are only permitted to 'guess' at McClellan's strength, but you may safely put it at 40 per cent. more than his opponents,' and the siege train I know to be unexampled. When at Fortress Monroe in January last, I saw several acres of ground covered with heavy ordnance, most of the guns being of 6-inch to 9-inch calibre, and these were all waiting to be rifled at the workshops lately established there. From all I can gather, the attack will not take place for ten days or a fortnight—the armies under Burnside, McDowell, Banks, and Fremont, being first required to take up certain positions. I believe the new iron ship 'Galena' will co-operate with McClellan in the assault on the enemy's works, part of Commodore Goldsborough's squadron assisting her.

The Western armies, under Halleck, Grant, and Buell, are dealing fearful blows upon the enemy on the northern frontier of the cotton States. One hundred continuous miles of the Memphis and Charleston railroad are now in possession of the Federal commanders, thus destroying the communications between Virginia and the Valley of the Mississippi; and simultaneously with this two long bridges have been removed on the Mobile and Ohio Railroad. General Halleck has taken supreme command in person of the armies under Grant and Buell, largely increasing their numbers by new reinforcements, and we are daily expecting intelligence of an attack on the enemy's lines at Corinth. We are getting the truth of the two days' battle at Pittsburg Landing, or Shiloh, as the Confederates call it. The first day was a splendid success for Beauregard, but Monday decided the contest in favour of the North. This is now admitted by the rebels themselves, as will be seen by the correspondence between Beauregard and Grant after the battle. So far as the number of prisoners is concerned, and also the capture of artillery, the advantage appears to be largely in favour of the Confederates; but the latter in their retreat left behind them vast quantities of arms, ammunition and caissons, and they must now be suffering from partial demoralisation. It may be Halleck's intention not to attack them at Corinth, until they are still further disheartened by the fall of Memphis. Commodore Foote and General Pope are now bombarding Fort Pillow, some miles above the city, and when it falls nothing more will intervene than Fort Randolph, neither of them being very strong.

The capture of Fort Pulaski, at the mouth of the Savannah river, clears the way for Dupont's gunboats to Fort Jackson, a work which must surrender after a few hours' bombardment. The Federal army is now within eight miles of the city of Savannah, and with Dupont thundering on its river front, they will not be long in clearing out its defenders. I should not be surprised at the place surrendering without striking a blow. There now remain but two United States' forts on the Atlantic coast in the hands of the rebels—Fort Sumter, in Charleston harbour, and Fort Macon, near Beaufort, North Carolina. Burnside has nearly completed his batteries on the islands surrounding the latter, and, when they open fire, the fort must quickly surrender.

It is pleasant to turn from these scenes of bloodshed to the peaceful events now transpiring in this capital of the American Union. The President has to-day signed the Bill of Emancipation in the District of Columbia, after a hesitation which still further proves the goodness of his heart and his far-seeing statesmanship. He expresses his fears to Congress that their newly acquired freedom may injure some of the negroes, and he suggests a supplemental bill in favour of 'minors, *femmes covertes*, insane, or absent persons.' It is asserted here that Mr. Lincoln consulted no adviser previous to signing this bill, and that up to the moment of sending his special message to Congress nobody knew what his action would be on the question.

The value of a slave is fixed by this Act at 300 dollars, rather a falling off in the price of 'chattels' on eight months ago. It is, however, an immense increase on the estimates of Southern planters. When a coloured child is born, his owner enters 100 dollars to his own credit in his cash-book, and when a negro dies—no matter what his assumed value may have been—he enters 100 dollars on the other side of the account. There is one clause in the Act which is likely to meet with misconstruction in Europe—namely, the appropriation for colonising the freed slaves. This was adopted to silence the weak-nerved, whose name is legion, and to enable any of the slaves who see fit to emigrate to more genial climes. The measure, notwithstanding, is an extremely bitter pill to the residents of this city and the inhabitants of Maryland, and still more so to the numerous Irish population. I heard a newsboy this evening crying out, 'Second edition of the *Star*; all the niggers our equals,' in a partially Celtic accent, very much to the amusement of the by-standers, for the Irish have always proved themselves inimical to the coloured race. This may be accounted for by the fact of their learning from their pro-slavery democratic leaders that if the negroes are set free they will soon decrease the scale of wages; and yet these very men assert that the negroes will not work! It is rumoured that the 'coloured folk' are organising a grand procession, 'break-down' and jubilee in honour of their emancipa-

tion, and that the Irish swear they will break up the
fête if they attempt it. I am quite sure the authorities
will not permit the rejoicings to be interfered with so long
as the negroes conduct themselves as peaceable and well-
disposed people.

April 18.

We have further news from Yorktown. The enemy has
attempted a midnight attack upon McClellan's lines; but
his forces being on the *qui vive*, and much more numerous than the assailants, the sortie was repulsed. Jefferson
Davis has arrived at the scene of operations, and assumed
command in chief of the rebels. We shall probably have
a decisive battle there in the course of next week, and
I trust to be there, and get off with a whole skin.

There is considerable excitement here relative to the
visit of M. Mercier, the French Minister, to Norfolk, and
the expected arrival of a French frigate below this city.
It is rumoured among the *quidnuncs* that the object of
the Minister's trip is to advise the insurgents, on the part
of his Imperial master, to submit themselves to the
Federal Government. The tone of French residents in
Washington has lately changed wonderfully, and it is
asserted that their Government is preparing to revoke
its recognition of the belligerent rights of the Confederates. Perhaps! I trust, however, that England will be
beforehand with the Emperor in such action as this.

The report that Porter's mortar-fleet has entered the
Mississippi and passed Forts Jackson and Philip without
their firing a shot, is regarded as a newspaper *canard* by
well-informed people. Porter, I am able to state on authority, is now on his way to the point in question, and may
ere this have arrived at his destination, but the Navy

Department has received no information whatever of the fact. Butler is also on his way from Ship Island and Pass Christian into Lake Pontchartrain, and we shall shortly hear of New Orleans being attacked in front and rear simultaneously. It is believed here that the city of Savannah is already in possession of General Hunter.

April 26.

After some difficulty, I have at length been successful in obtaining a pass to join and accompany the army of the Potomac, on the Yorktown Peninsula. For several days past, I despaired of accomplishing this object: officer after officer whom I was advised to see, informed me that he had no power to grant my request, and referred me to somebody else who always told me the same story. Thus marched from one to another, I finally discovered that it would be necessary for me to seek an interview with the Secretary of War; but just there was the difficulty, for Secretaries of War are usually surrounded with subordinates, who desire to know your business before admitting you to the presence of the great official. I managed at length to penetrate the *enceinte,* and did not find Mr. Stanton the gruff, disagreeable personage he is so generally represented. He listened silently, but kindly, to the story of my difficulties with his subordinates, and finally wrote me a pass with his own hand.

My English friends here regard me as wonderfully lucky, whilst I credit my success to the fair and honourable tone adopted by the paper I represent in dealing with American affairs.

CHAPTER VII.

THE YORKTOWN PENINSULA.

FORTRESS MONROE, VIRGINIA: April 30.

THE 'Merrimac' has not made her appearance since my last, and it is thought that additions are being made to her hull which will require some time to complete. We hear that her iron armour is to be extended some two feet lower down, but naval officers doubt the truth of this rumour, as such an improvement would necessitate her lying in dock for many weeks. The 'Merrimac,' be it understood, is a fair-weather vessel, and her constitution cannot stand easterly winds; when the wind comes from the east, a strong sea sets in through the mouth of the Chesapeake Bay, and the Confederate battery engaging the 'Monitor' or any other antagonist would expose her wooden bottom while rolling. Perhaps the true explanation of her absence these many days lies in the fact that iron ports are being added to her: hitherto her port-holes have been open, and it is found that fragments of shell, grape, &c. enter her decks, and necessarily interfere with the working of her guns. The preparations made to receive her are considerable, and, maybe, the enemy have obtained some information upon the matter and are afraid to let her venture out. Within a mile from this shore lie the 'Monitor,' 'Naugatuck,' and 'Galena,' all iron-plated batteries mounting the heaviest of guns, and at easy distances are the 'Vanderbilt' and other ocean mail steamers, ready to rush in upon her should she run the gauntlet of the former. Perhaps, too, the approach of the army under General Burnside has something to do with her remaining at home, and it may be, after all, that the 'Monitor' will have to run the enemy's shore batteries on the Elizabeth River in order to reach her old antagonist.

I passed a pleasant hour this morning on board Ericsson's wonderful little vessel, and the more I see of her the more astonishing she appears; she is, in fine, the pet of all here—soldiers, sailors, and civilians alike, and great dissatisfaction is expressed that she was not permitted to steam in and finish off the 'Merrimac' at the latter's last appearance. Lieutenant Jeffers, her commander, is on the *qui vive* the whole time, and most anxious to test the improvements made upon his vessel since her fight; her wheel-house, which was formerly the weakest part, is now if anything stronger than the turret, and no such accident can again occur as that which so injured Lieutenant Worden. An inspection of the wheel-house would satisfy the most incredulous of the superiority of successive plates, one upon the other, over single solid blocks of iron. The house in question is built up with blocks of the best hammered iron nine inches thick, and yet one of these was broken in half by a rifle shot, leaving a crack on the rear side three-eighths of an inch wide. When the turret was struck in a similar manner the outside plate, although but an inch thick, was merely indented, and the deck, a single plate of inch iron, suffered no worse. The injury would scarcely be noticed until pointed out.

After leaving the 'Monitor' I went on board the

'Galena,' which is simply an ordinary sloop of war iron-plated, and although much stronger than anything until lately heard of, yet is by no means to be compared with the 'Monitor.' Her sides incline inwards at an apparent angle of twenty degrees, giving her when looking 'bow on' a very wicked appearance; the spar deck is narrow, and covered from stem to stern with inch iron. This is strong enough to resist the ricochetting of any projectiles, no matter how heavy, and the only thing which can hurt it would be heavy shell thrown from mortars. These batteries, however, are intended for close quarters, where it would be impossible to obtain sufficient elevation to strike the deck at right angles. The port-holes of the 'Galena' are simply those of a ship of war iron plated, and are moved up and down on their hinges by tackling. Her commander, Captain John Rodgers, however, says he shall fight her with open ports, and take his chances of being damaged by the enemy's shot. The ports of the 'Monitor' are pendular and inside the turret, and the batteries now constructing will have theirs formed after this same fashion. The gun deck of the 'Galena' presents a very unsightly appearance from the great number of bolt-heads, and these are likely to cause much confusion and injury during action; her commander is guarding against this eventuality by covering up the walls with strong canvas and oakum.

Stevens's little model, called the 'Naugatuck,' is almost as interesting an object as the strange-looking 'Monitor,' and is well deserving the attention of naval constructors. She exemplifies three new principles, the power of rapid submersion, increased speed combined with rapidity of turning and loading the guns by machinery. She is a little craft of some 150 tons, wooden built, but her bow covered with iron armour; when in action, the heads of her gunners have two feet and a half of water over them, and they may therefore be considered out of danger. The 'Naugatuck' carries one 100-pounder Parrott rifle-gun, thirteen feet long, and weighing nearly 10,000 lbs.; this gun is fixed on the vessel's deck in the line of the keel, and is trained at an object by pointing, not the gun, but the vessel herself. Of course it is not intended to work guns in this manner hereafter, the object being merely to prove the power of the battery in turning rapidly on her centre, but her commander informs me that the gun can be brought to bear upon an object in very much less time than by the ordinary method. The recoil is taken up by india-rubber springs—an invention also of Mr. Stevens. The trunnions work in a square iron block, which runs on a solid iron *châssis*, or way, and sixteen vulcanised india-rubber bricks, two inches thick, are compressed by the recoil, and send the gun back to its former position, where it is again met by blocks of rubber, and held to its place. The charge of powder is from ten to fifteen pounds, but the recoil never exceeds thirteen inches. Should it be necessary to change the india-rubber, this can be effected almost instantaneously by withdrawing a pin and putting in new bricks. The loading of the gun is another peculiarity; the muzzle is lowered beneath the deck, the charge hoisted to it on a platform, and rammed home by machinery. In the new Stevens' Battery all this will be done by steam, but on board the 'Naugatuck' tackling is employed, and proves to be far more rapid than the ordinary method of loading guns. Mr. Stevens proved by actual experiment that no more time is required to load any gun, no matter of what calibre, than is sufficient for turning a steam-cock twice—once to raise the charge to the muzzle, and once to let the steam upon the piston which rams it home. The day is evidently not far distant when ships of war will do almost everything by machinery, and in that case the best mechanics will necessarily be the best sailors.

May 1.

3 P.M.—The wind has changed from easterly to southwest, and as the water is consequently placid almost as a mirror, we are in high expectations of a visit from the 'Merrimac' and her consorts the 'Jamestown' and 'Yorktown.' The 'Monitor,' 'Galena,' and 'Naugatuck' have their steam up, and numerous are the telescopes directed towards Sewall's Point, where the enemy's ships first make their appearance.

Nothing of importance has passed before Yorktown during the past three days, and, from all I can learn, the present week will go over without McClellan's attempting any active movement. The impression seems to be that M'Dowell, Banks, and Fremont will first take up certain positions menacing Richmond, thus necessitating the withdrawal of part of the enemy's force; but whether this be the intention or not, outsiders are never permitted to learn. General Wool signed my pass to McClellan's lines yesterday, and I intend leaving Fortress Monroe to-morrow for the mouth of the York River, in order to take up my quarters permanently with the army. The roads, I learn, are still almost impassable, even for horses; but the hot summer's sun of to-day will render them somewhat drier, although a week of fine weather is necessary to make them of the required consistence. I hope to see another engagement with the 'Merrimac,' however, between this and to-morrow noon, the hour when the steamer leaves Fortress Monroe for Shipping Point.

4 P.M.—General Wool, commanding this department, has just received information of the fall of Fort Macon, North Carolina. The capture of this stronghold gives the Federal Government entire possession of the coast of that State, and Burnside is henceforward free to march upon Norfolk. General Wool learns also, by flag of truce from the latter place, that the officers of the 'Merrimac' have been sent to Yorktown, and that the battery will remain at her present anchorage in order to protect the dockyard. It is more than possible that this is merely a *ruse*, on the part of the enemy, to lull suspicion. I am also informed that Beauregard has fallen back from Corinth upon Memphis. He will not long be able to hold this position, for the capture of New Orleans leaves Porter and Farragut free to enter the Mississippi river with their fleets, and to effect a junction with Foote's squadron. From New Orleans to Memphis there are few, if any, batteries, the banks being generally low and swampy; we may therefore look for the early annihilation of the western rebel army, and the reduction of the valley of the Mississippi to the Federal rule before hot weather sets in.

CHEESEMAN'S CREEK, SOUTHERN VIRGINIA: May 2.

Thinking there was small likelihood of the reappearance of the 'Merrimac,' I left Fortress Monroe this morning at 10 A.M., and after a pleasant steamboat ride of two hours reached the above busy spot in the vicinity of Yorktown. Another visit to General Wool put me in possession of further particulars relating to the 'Merrimac.' Commodore Tatnall—who is already known to your readers as the flag-officer of the 'Mosquito Fleet' in the South Carolina waters, but whose occupation has lately been interfered with by Commodore Dupont's squadron—has commanded the 'Merrimac' since her engagement with the 'Monitor;' an order given him some days ago to run the gauntlet of the shipping and batteries in Hampton Roads, and to make his way to the York River, was demurred to on the plea of insufficient depth of water, and on the order being emphasised he immediately tendered his resignation. Lieutenant Catesby Jones, the second in command, adopted the same action, and the vessel is therefore without officers for the present. This information, obtained from 'contrabands,' may or may not be correct, but the Southern papers relieve us of all doubt as to the resignations, while the explanation has, at all events, the appearance of truth, except in regard to the depth of water. York River is a broad and deep stream, but the 'Monitor' is an antagonist not to be mastered or evaded.

Cheeseman's Creek is a branch of the Poquosin, which empties itself into Chesapeake Bay a few miles south of York River. It would be difficult to make Europeans understand by mere description the beauty of these Southern bays and harbours, broad and deep streams emptying themselves in almost countless numbers along the entire coast. Maps must be drawn on a considerable scale to give half their names. As usual, however, Southern *insouciance*, or, as we should call it, laziness, has turned none of these natural advantages to account, and, if what I hear be true, no steamer ever ruffled the placid waters of this creek until the arrival of Heintzelman's *corps d'armée* four weeks ago. I was unprepared for the scene which presented itself as we left the Chesapeake and steered towards the landing: ocean steamers, river steamers from all the Northern cities, tug-boats, ships, schooners, flat-boats, &c., in amazing numbers, and a perfect forest of masts far away inland. We steamed through them for nearly four miles, and had it not been for those immense floating villages which so excite the astonishment of foreigners, I might have supposed we were in our 'Pool.' Not one of the vessels, however, but is here on business of the army, all supplies from the North coming to this point. On the improvised docks thousands of soldiers are engaged in landing stores; 100-pounder rifled guns, mortars of all sizes up to 13 inch, shot, shell, biscuit, barrels, flour, pork—in fact, an *olla podrida* of everything useable by an army bestrews the shore for miles. Long unbroken lines of white-top army wagons roll carelessly towards the woods; camps meet the eye on every point, and the excitement is increased by the music of different bands, and the distant booming of artillery at Yorktown. I learn from a friend in the 1st New Jersey Brigade, temporarily encamped at this point, that the heavy guns are only fired by the enemy, we replying occasionally with field-pieces alone; the object being to prevent the Confederates knowing the position of the works until the bombardment commences in earnest. At night-time the firing is continuous, doubtless to hinder our working parties engaged in mounting the siege guns along the fourteen miles of batteries and entrenchments.

The 1st Jersey Brigade forms part of Franklin's division, and really belongs therefore to the *corps d'armée* of General M'Dowell. McClellan, however, made a special demand for this division some weeks ago, and after considerable trouble obtained it. From all I can gather, it is destined for special service at no very remote period—no less than an attack in conjunction with the fleet upon Gloucester Point, directly opposite Yorktown, on the York River. We are of course unaware of the enemy's strength at the point in question, but as Franklin's command is about equal to our army at the Alma, and that ten 13-inch mortars and a proportionate amount of other ordnance will be carried thither, added to the fact of the major portion of Commodore Goldborough's fleet acting in conjunction with the land forces, we may safely presume that the enemy is not to be dislodged easily. Gloucester Point is less than a mile from Yorktown, and the question presents itself whether McClellan will take this point first, or wait until his preparations are completed along the entire breadth of the peninsula. I may be able to discover this to-morrow.

CHAPTER VIII.

IN FRONT OF YORKTOWN.

CAMP OF THE 105TH PENNSYLVANIA, NEAR YORKTOWN: May 3.

A HARD day's work has given me much valuable information relative to the progress of this siege. Calling upon General Seth Williams, the Acting Adjutant-General of the army, I learned from him that no civilians are permitted to enter the trenches, or to pass beyond the lines of main guard—in fact, no officer can pass the latter without special authorisation from the Commander-in-Chief; and so strictly is this rule enforced, that many have been placed in arrest for attempting to infringe it. Otherwise every facility has been extended to me, and I am now placed on the same footing as the gentlemen representing American papers.

The approach to the head-quarters of the army is really very beautiful, and greatly enhanced by the first blushes of early spring. The only thing to mar my pleasure was the villanous roads, if such they may be called, for Virginia's attention has not been much devoted to improving her means of inter-communication. Mud, mud everywhere, except where the Northern soldiers have *corduroy'd* the route by placing pine-trees side by side, and strewing saplings on the top. In this manner they have transplanted guns weighing 17,000 lbs. a distance of twelve miles, and supplies reach an army of more than a hundred thousand men daily in the same manner.

Surely there can be no doubt of the efficiency of the Quartermaster's and Commissary's departments after the statement of the above fact, and yet these immense stores have first to be brought to the Northern ports, then shipped a distance of 200 or 300 miles, landed in the enemy's country, and carried in wagons over roads made by the army itself. What other nation has ever embarked at once an army of upwards of 100,000 men, provided, too, with far more and heavier ordnance than even France has employed? I may hereafter be permitted to give you a list of the guns brought hither, but I know already of one battery of fifteen rifled 100-pounders, each piece weighing nearly 10,000 lbs.; and I have visited another this afternoon mounting five of the same calibre, besides two 200-pounders. A Hungarian officer who has served sixteen years in the Austrian Artillery, assures me that no European army ever brought so many field-pieces into the field with a single army; and, for the matter of that, the whole country for miles appears to be covered with artillery camps.

General McClellan's head-quarters are situated on a magnificent plateau in the midst of, I should judge, 30,000 men. Less than two miles in front are the enemy's works at Yorktown, and the busy scene is greatly enhanced in interest by the frequent reports of his guns, and the bursting of an occasional shell in the trees. Were they at all cognisant of the location of these camps they would necessarily make the situation unpleasant, but high trees intervene and their shots are merely thrown at random. Steam sawmills are hard at work all round turning out material for the fortifications; and facing the General's camp, about a quarter of a mile forward, Professor Lowe's new balloon hides itself behind the woods or mounts in the air for a few minutes' reconnaissance. A little to the right we obtain a good view of the famous York River, and if we walk half a mile further on we can see Yorktown and Gloucester Point and the long line of the enemy's water batteries. Creeks and small rivers cut the prospect into a very network of beauty, and my glass shows me companies of men in the distance building bridges, and trains of wagons passing to and fro in all directions. It is a panorama far too grand and extended for words to describe accurately.

In company with two gentlemen representing a daily and illustrated paper of New York city, I called upon General Heintzelman, an officer commanding a *corps d'armée* of some 40,000 men. The General received us in the most friendly way imaginable, chatting with us for perhaps half an hour. One of his remarks struck me as most important, going far to prove, as it does, the immense value of these new iron-plated ships. 'I would sooner,' said he, 'know that the "Merrimac" was taken or sunk than have this army (meaning McClellan's) reinforced by 60,000 men;' and he gave solid reasons for his opinion too. The large force thrown upon Yorktown, numbering upwards of 100,000 troops, receives all its supplies down the James and York rivers, and the Federal gunboats dare not venture far up these streams, fearing that the dreaded destroyer may issue forth and treat them as she did the 'Cumberland' and the 'Congress.' The officers have full confidence in the superior strength and capabilities of the 'Monitor,' but something may go wrong with her, and they have then no other safety than shallow water and a wide berth. It is simply a fact that the

'Merrimac,' at Norfolk, blockades the James and York rivers, and yet the mouth of the latter is forty miles away from that harbour.

Having obtained permission to visit a newly finished battery on the banks of the York River, we bade adieu to the General, and sallied forth in the direction of the camp of Berdan's sharpshooters. This regiment is formed of picked marksmen, selected from different States, and I learn that the crack shots are either Minnesota, Wisconsin, or other Western men, and Vermonters or citizens of New Hampshire—men in fine who have been weaned on rifles, and get most of their meals by shooting for them. Four companies are from New York, and one is composed of Tyrolese; but the crack individual shot is an elderly original who goes by the name of 'California Joe.' He is said to have brought down more than a score of the enemy from his pit, and is represented never to miss his aim in any instance. The rifle used is what we know as the Swiss, some of them weighing twenty-five pounds, but every man is drilled in the use of his particular choice weapon, and avails himself of rests, telescopes, &c. All the army bears witness to the invaluable services rendered by these experienced riflemen, and the fame of their deeds now extends over the entire country. Their camp is a model of beauty, every company pitching its tents in an avenue of evergreens and flowers, and visitors entering the inclosure by triumphal arches of different designs. The whizzing sound of an occasional shell falling near or beyond the camp lends a piquant relish of danger to the otherwise peaceful scene.

A walk of two miles over hills, through valleys, and across numerous bridges lately constructed, brought us finally to the house where Cornwallis and Washington signed the capitulation of York Town, situated on the high banks of the York River, and giving a splendid view of York Town and Gloucester Point. In what was formerly the back garden of the house, the 1st Connecticut Volunteer Artillery have thrown up a battery mounting seven guns—five 100-pounders, and two 200—all of them cast and rifled on the Parrott principle. We first entered the deserted building and established ourselves on the top story, whence we obtained an admirable view of the enemy's water battery, under the bluff on which York Town is situated. Our battery had just commenced firing, and the enemy was replying at the first about gun for gun, theirs being evidently of heavy calibre. The distance was about two miles, across water—perhaps a little over, even —and we presented a far better mark than they, being not merely on a hill, but in the bright sunshine, whilst they were in the shade. Their shots generally fell short; but at last we heard a loud report, and the whizzing, fluttering noise of a shell, which flew screaming towards us in a direct line, and fell into the water only about 100 yards in front of us. As they would probably give the piece a trifle more elevation the next shot, we judged it discreet to descend into the battery, whence we watched the contest at our ease for half an hour. I had the pleasure of meeting here the Hon. John Tucker, the Assistant-Secretary of War. He expressed himself very pleased both with the range of the guns and the excellence of the firing, and certainly the latter could with difficulty be surpassed. A young gentleman, who but lately joined the regiment from civil life, trained and sighted a piece, and the shell fell in the river close to the enemy's position. He then called for an eighteen-seconds' fuse, and, firing the second time, he landed the shell clean in the rebel battery, an enormous geyser of sand and earth rising where it fell. Three other shots from different guns produced exactly the same effect, and we could see the enemy scattering in all directions. When we left, that battery was silenced. I am given to understand that a gun of heavy calibre and great range burst lately in this work of the Confederates, and was shown fragments of the conical shell picked up in a field one quarter of a mile beyond this point; these fragments prove it to be of the Blakeley manufacture, and there are many such in the rebel States. Several were taken by Dupont in Florida. The range of the 100-pound Parrott gun (rifled) is $4\frac{1}{2}$ miles, and I much doubt whether its accuracy can be exceeded. It is a muzzle-loader, like all American guns.

Retracing our steps, we were invited to take tea with the major of a Pennsylvania cavalry regiment camped in a thick wood. The major related a circumstance to us which admirably exemplifies the utter want of energy of these slave-State men, their pride and downright stupidity. On the outskirts of the wood there resides a farmer, who is about the only native who has not run away since the approach of the Northern army; the cavalry have thrown their manure in heaps upon his land, and perhaps a couple of acres are covered with the mounds lying close to each other. A few days ago the major asked the farmer why he did not grow more than one stick of Indian corn upon a hill. 'Why,' said he, doggedly, 'the ground's too poor.' 'But,' remarked the officer, 'we are now manuring it for you, and we shall very soon cover in the whole of your farm.' 'Oh,' replied the Virginian, 'that won't do any good, I haven't got any fences.' 'Why, then,' said the major, 'do you not get up early in the morning and fell a lot of young pines, so as to make a rail fence?' The farmer demurred to this as derogatory to his position to work, although assured he should be protected from all interference. And yet of such stuff is the people formed who are now raving about independence of the South!

I am writing from the camp of the 105th Pennsylvanian Volunteers, a little in the rear of General McClellan's quarters, at eleven o'clock p.m. The enemy is keeping up a most vigorous cannonading in front of us, hoping to stop our working parties. The woods behind us re-echo the noise of the guns and screaming of the shell, making them appear quite close to us instead of three miles or so off. Musketry at this hour, however, would be infinitely more startling, but I think the enemy is scarcely likely to make any night sortie.

CHAPTER IX.

EVACUATION OF YORKTOWN.

May 4, 8.0 A.M.

A NEGRO came into camp this morning, bringing news of the evacuation of Yorktown by the rebel army. This was, of course, discredited until confirmed by the signal corps and advanced pickets, and we now hear that the Stars and Stripes float over the deserted town. The feeling amongst the troops is that of bitter disappointment, shared in by officers and men alike; for there is an universal opinion wherever I have been during the past hour and a half that they are outrageously 'sold,' and their leaders utterly incompetent. 'We came here to fight,' they say, 'not to turn ditchers; and we might have bagged the whole crowd inside Yorktown weeks ago, if McClellan had had the pluck.' The evacuation will, of course, be heralded as a great Union success, but the army calls it by a very different name.

4.0 P.M.

I am now writing on board the steamboat 'Hero,' which is lying out in stream on the edge of the Chesapeake. Where our destination is we can only surmise, the general impression being that we shall land near Norfolk. The whole of Franklin's division is about to leave for parts unknown, and we are momentarily expecting orders to depart.

The enemy have left all their heavy guns, a portion of their camp equipage, and large quantities of commissary stores; they blew up their magazine before leaving. Through information obtained from stragglers and contrabands, it appears their men had become demoralised on hearing of the fall of New Orleans and Fort Macon, in North Carolina, and their officers could no longer place confidence in them. The retreat commenced on Thursday, and their heavy cannonading of the past five days was simply to mask their movements; if they have also evacuated their water batteries on the York River we shall reach them before they get far distant.

Colonel Key, of McClellan's staff, states his impression, which is very probably the conviction also of the General himself, that the Confederate army has retreated to the Chickahominy River.

We have rumours of grand successes under Halleck in the West, but the particulars are withheld from the public; if that General and McClellan can only get in the rear of the retreating armies, the horrors of a guerilla campaign will be avoided. Halleck will do so, for Pope, with 35,000 men, and Mitchell, with 30,000, have by this time effected a junction of their forces south of the latitude of Memphis. Rely upon it Burnside is not idle in North Carolina, and I hazard the prediction that neither Beauregard's army in the West, nor that under Davis and Johnstone, will ever reach the cotton States except as demoralised stragglers. It is known to the authorities at Washington that Governor Clark, of North Carolina, has been arrested as a traitor to the Confederate Government, and carried prisoner to Richmond, the charge being made of his having offered to surrender his state to Burnside. North Carolina is far more Union than any other member of the so-called

Confederacy, and should it enter into McClellan's plan to occupy her territory, he will receive every assistance from her citizens. I expect to see a large force precipitated forthwith upon Weldon and to the westward, our command of the sea and the interior waters giving us an immense advantage over the enemy. The question now is, Where are the Confederates about making a stand? M'Dowell has finished his bridge over the Rappahannock, and is fast advancing upon Richmond; and Banks will not be long in effecting a junction with him and Fremont. All the cavalry and flying artillery of this army are now hastening after the retreaters, and McClellan may, by this time, have obtained information so as to modify his plans to meet the new exigencies of the case.

10.0 P.M.

The captain of our steamboat has just received orders to be ready to leave at half-past three in the morning, and bets are in favour of Lynn Haven, near Norfolk, as our destination. Fifteen or more large steamers, each carrying a thousand men, lie near our moorings, and a perfect fleet of brigs and schooners surround the larger craft.

YORK RIVER, OPPOSITE YORKTOWN: May 5, 6.0 A.M.

The whole of Franklin's division is now lying off this place in steamers; gunboats are in front of us, and our troops throng both sides of the stream. We are waiting for the order to leave, the rain again falling in torrents. I must close this letter, in the hopes of it reaching New York in time for Wednesday's steamer.

YORKTOWN, VIRGINIA: May 5, 8 P.M.

We have lain here all day, momentarily expecting the order to move. My friend, Colonel Torbert of the 1st

New Jersey infantry, has just received instructions to weigh anchor at midnight, and proceed up the river to West Point, in company with the rest of the brigade, and Franklin's division. The latter numbers some 16,000 men, and we shall, within the next twelve hours, have landed that force, plentifully supplied with artillery, in the rear of the retreating Confederates. The distance from Yorktown to West Point, at the head of the York River, is, by water, some thirty miles, and a railroad, some forty miles long, leads thence to Richmond. The retreating Confederates are evidently endeavouring to reach this terminus so as to transport their artillery and heavy stores to Petersburg, and thence, south. Query—will they do it? Magruder, we now know for certain, commenced his backward movement on Thursday, and perhaps his advance has already reached West Point. We, on the other hand, have the advantage of this deep and wide river, and our gunboats are worth 50,000 men to us. There is a rumour that Banks and M'Dowell have just taken, and are now occupying, Richmond. If this be correct, although I doubt it, the enemy is hemmed in on this peninsula, and must fight from desperation or surrender; but the question depends on the chances of our getting in the enemy's rear, or the presence of Banks and M'Dowell at Richmond. All day the rain has fallen in torrents, and the roads must be in an impassable condition for artillery; this, however, will be less damaging to McClellan than to the enemy, for he has command of the river and its tributaries.

Camp rumours, the stupidest of *canards*, tell to-day of serious reverses to our troops while attacking the rear of the retreating Confederates at Williamsburg.* We hear

---

* See p. 106.

of six batteries of field-artillery captured, and three colonels taken prisoners, but the report is on no better authority than the word of an orderly. One thing, however, is certain; numbers of our men have been wounded or killed by torpedoes placed in the road, and the feeling of the troops is naturally much incensed against an antagonist who resorts to such unworthy means. The rapid advance of the cavalry and flying artillery soon came up with the enemy, and the impression is general that the entire body of the main army of the rebels is still on the peninsula.

I went on shore this morning, with the hope of inspecting the deserted fortifications, but found that no one under the grade of general officer was permitted to enter without a special pass. Expecting an order to move, I returned to the steamer, meeting on the shore the captain of the French frigate 'Gassendi.' He told me the 'Merrimac' was out in the James River, and he was hastening back to Fortress Monroe, expecting to witness another engagement between her and the 'Monitor.' The captain was present at the *début* of the 'Merrimac,' and has inspected her thoroughly above and below, as also her little antagonist. He gives the opinion that the former would prove the more powerful in deep water and the 'Monitor' in shallow, but I am afraid he may possess some of the prejudices against change which old salts so generally evince. I believe it will be found that the 'Merrimac' is out in order to blockade the James River, so as to cover the passage of the retreating Confederates. I hear that Captain Fox, the Assistant-Secretary of the Navy, is at Fortress Monroe, and I hope, therefore, that the 'Monitor' and 'Galena' will receve permission to engage her.

WEST POINT, VIRGINIA: May 6.

We left Yorktown this morning at eight o'clock, the entire of Franklin's division sailing at the same time, and presenting an imposing appearance on the magnificent York River. This stream is almost as straight and even in breadth as a canal, and the banks are more thickly settled than any Southern river I have yet seen. Perhaps this is owing to the beauty of the country through which it runs—a beauty much resembling that of our Thames above Kew and Richmond. The exclamations of delight at the scenery were general amongst both officers and men, and numbers promised themselves a farm on the banks of York River as soon as the war is over. Nothing interfered with our passage to the head of the stream, nor did anything offer which could excite our interest, and we reached West Point after a very quiet and slow passage between four and five o'clock in the evening. West Point is the south-eastern extremity of the tongue of land formed by the Pamunkey and Mattapony rivers, and from it runs a railroad to Richmond, which the retreating rebels are endeavouring to reach.

I have obtained some particulars relative to the evacuation of the rebel lines at Yorktown from officers who inspected them yesterday. From the assertions of stragglers and Confederate prisoners, it would appear that the enemy were perfectly unprepared for the heavy artillery brought against them; and they preferred to evacuate in time, rather than hazard the bombardment which would have opened last Monday. Their own works were admirably well constructed, and we should have had difficulty and great loss of life in carrying them. The two points of Yorktown and Gloucester Point, 1,000 yards apart, and both fortified down to the water's edge, kept the gunboats at a respectful distance; but our guns were of heavier calibre and of much greater range than their own, and they left everything to us which they had taken months to collect. The guns evidently defended the shores of York River at an early period, for the batteries are overgrown with long, thick grass.

On the dock at Yorktown we found two of our 200lb. Parrott rifle shot, unexploded, packed in boxes to forward to Richmond. One was labelled as follows:— 'This was *throwned* (sic) from a land battery at the mouth of Wormley Creek, belonging to the Yankees; distance four and a half miles. Time, two o'clock, April 30, 1862.' The second was marked thus:—' From a Yankee steamer; distance five miles.' The Confederate prisoners in our hands express the greatest astonishment at the range of our heavy guns; in places where shell have fallen they have driven a post into the ground, and written particulars similar to the above. I learn from one of our principal artillery officers that shot fired from our battery at Wormley Creek passed completely over Yorktown into the country beyond—a distance of between five and six miles.

CHAPTER X.

BATTLE OF WEST POINT, VA.

May 7, 9 P.M.

WE have been fighting all day since 8 A.M., and the gunboats are still throwing shell into the enemy's lines. Although as tired as a man needs be, I must chronicle the events of the past twelve hours before courting the blankets, believing that those of the morrow will be still more exciting. We have been attacked by the enemy in force, and remain masters of the field.

The armies under Generals Lee and Magruder are now endeavouring to reach Richmond by the road running the length of the peninsula, the north-western extremity passing by West Point. McClellan is following them up, his advance treading on their very heels; and, if what we hear be correct, he is now less than ten miles' distance from this place. The position of the army under General Franklin is on the southern shores of the mouth of the Pamunkey River—not at West Point itself—and the road the retreating rebels are following passes within three miles of our encampment. It will thus be seen that we are in a position to outflank them and cut off their retreat; an operation which will probably be attempted to-morrow when our reinforcements have arrived. The rebels, imagining very properly that we were in comparatively small force, hoped to drive us into the river; and, were it not for the peculiar position taken up by General Franklin, they might have succeeded. Our little army is camping on a broad plain at the head of the York River, and dense woods and swamps intervene between the contending forces, the edge of this almost impassable forest forming a semicircle, the ends of which rest on the water. A good broad road runs from the centre of the arc through the woods to the route traversed by the foe whom McClellan is following up the peninsula, and there is a distance of about a mile and a half from that centre to the water. We have thus a broad and level plain on which to manœuvre an army of at least 30,000 men, and a position, too, in which an army may defend itself successfully against almost any numbers, because the enemy can bring forward neither cavalry nor artillery. Add to this the presence of the gunboats enfilading the approaches, and you will admit that the Confederates are justified in regarding us as dangerous neighbours. It is quite probable that their retreat upon Richmond will be prevented, and, if so, they cannot easily reach the railroads running towards the Gulf States.

The first intimation given us of the enemy's attack was by a negro who approached our pickets in the woods early this morning. He informed the officer in command of the intended advance, stating at the same time that General Lee was only about three miles distant from us, and that we should be attacked almost immediately. The first sound of musketry was heard a little before eight o'clock, and told of a large force in the woods: the different regiments did not wait for orders from the general-in-command, but formed into line instanter, with an alacrity which proved how much their hearts were in the struggle. The sound came from the left of the camp of the 1st New Jersey, and I immediately went down to head-quarters, where I found the whole of our artillery harnessing up, and aides-de-camp galloping about in all directions. General Franklin and staff were soon away towards that part of the woods whence the musketry proceeded, and were quickly followed by Hexamer's Jersey battery of six field-pieces, which dashed off in glorious style, with Platt's Napoleon guns hard on their heels. The infantry now began to move towards the woods at double quick, their bright rifles and bayonets reflecting, diamond-like, the sun's rays of a calm May morning. With an expedition that could not be surpassed, hospitals were established in different parts of the field, signal officers placed in trees, and a telegraph arranged from the front to the reserves, by stationing men within hailing distance of each other. I took up my own position on a rising ground in the centre of the plain, and had not merely a perfect view of the marchings and counter-marchings of the various regiments until they entered the woods, but heard the different reports brought in to General Slocum, second in command. I had not long been in this position when word was sent across the fields—'Brigade of enemy on our right!' A minute afterwards a third battery dashed away in the direction indicated, followed by its supports at double quick. We had scarcely turned our glasses towards the spot, vainly endeavouring to penetrate the thick forest wall, when shouts came again from the front of 'Enemy coming in on our left!' Out of the woods marched our skirmishers and pickets, driven in by a vastly superior force, and it seemed as though our little army were about to be surrounded by the entire force of the Confederates. Volleys of musketry succeeded each other rapidly, and the cry came over the field of 'The 95th are falling back!' This was a Pennsylvania regiment of Zouaves, and we soon had a number of their officers and men brought past us on stretchers, followed by more than a score stragglers covered with mud to their waists. The poor fellows had been on duty all night in the woods, and to escape from the enemy had to plunge through a morass, where many of them had stuck fast and were shot before they could extricate themselves. The attack finally resolved itself into one on our centre, where the road traverses the woods; when this became confirmed, the order was given for the infantry to fall back upon the open, and the batteries prepared to commence firing. A rebel regiment, the 5th Alabama, marched to the very edge of the woods, where they were received with a volley of double-shotted canister from the New Jersey battery, at the close range of 200 yards. The rest of the artillery immediately followed suit, changing the ammunition afterwards to shell; and when twenty-four pieces, aided by the gun-boats, had fully got into play, little was heard of the enemy for some two hours.

We received numerous reinforcements during the action, and towards afternoon, or rather evening, General Franklin found himself at the head of two divisions. This night and the morrow will bring him a third, and he will then be able to assume the offensive with an army of upwards of 40,000 men. Nearly all his regiments have moved forward into the woods, and at this hour (11 P.M.) they are bivouacking in close proximity to the enemy. I am writing this letter in the deserted camp of the 1st New Jersey, on the extreme right of our line, near the confluence of the Pamunkey with the York River. Every now and then the enemy fires towards the shipping from the direction of West Point, and the gunboats reply with their sonorous eleven-inch guns, waking up a thousand echoes in the woods. The sound, however, is in rather too close proximity to be altogether pleasant.

As usual in such cases, there have been many remarkable escapes. One man had the muzzle of his rifle carried away, the shot glancing downwards and grazing his thumb. A friend of mine, an officer on General Slocum's staff, rode right into the midst of the enemy, and, when turning to retreat, found himself in a shower of musket shot, one ball of which carried away the skin of his left ear and a lock of hair. Another, on General Newton's staff, also missed his way in the woods and came upon the enemy; they, taking him for a Confederate, asked him the whereabouts of Colonel Hampton, the commanding officer of a celebrated South Carolina regiment. He replied, with great presence of mind, 'Back here,' and immediately turned his horse's head; but a well-directed volley killed the animal, and he himself fell to the ground, feigning death. The rebels approached him, and proceeded to rifle his pockets, making several observations derogatory to Yankees in general, and himself in particular—so much so, in fact, that he broke out laughing, and they immediately marched him towards their lines. He had not gone many steps before a shell burst near to them, followed by a second in nearly the same place. 'Run,' said he, 'and I'll run, too;' and he did it, only in the opposite direction to his captors.

It is almost impossible to give a correct account of the killed and wounded in this engagement, but from all I can gather, I think 250 will cover our loss. The principal struggle was for possession of a certain fence away back in the woods, and the 31st and 32nd New York and 95th Pennsylvania suffered severely at this point. Supports coming up, they made a bayonet charge up to and over the fence, the enemy broke in confusion, and we are now holding the position with our pickets out beyond. I have heard no estimate of the enemy's casualties, but they were seen to carry off large numbers of killed and wounded. What their force was it would be vain to state, as they fought all the time, as they always do, under cover; but from the manner in which they drove us backwards until the artillery opened upon them, it is probable their numbers largely exceeded our own.

May 8.

The third division is disembarking from transports which arrived early this morning, and we have now upwards of 35,000 men on land. I learn that General McClellan has sent orders to Franklin to hold this position at all hazards until to-night, when he will be here in person. The regulars are on their way here, and all the reserve artillery as well. Franklin's division will be the vanguard of the advancing Federal army, and, as we are to leave our baggage, it is obviously intended to make forced marches upon the retreating enemy. In fact, it becomes a race between the two armies as to who shall first arrive at Richmond.

The Confederates retired during the night, but we are after them in force.

6 P.M.

We have employed this day in scouring the woods for killed and wounded, and preparing for an early departure. A second division, under command of General Sedgwick, has reinforced our army, and the advance guard of FitzJohn Porter's division is already here. We have now a force which, in conjunction with the gunboats, may defy any numbers the enemy can bring against us.

A walk to the General Hospital this morning satisfied

me more than ever of the atrocities of the rebels. I saw one of our dead brought in with a mortal wound in the chest, and his throat cut from ear to ear. Another poor fellow had his face smashed in by a blow from the butt end of a musket, or, which is more probable, by the heel of a man's boot, and the wound showed unmistakable evidence of having been inflicted when the sufferer lay on the ground. The effect upon the troops was immense—curses fierce being vented upon an enemy who could be guilty of such barbarities. I am sorry to say there is too much evidence of these cases being rather general than individual, as witness the torpedoes set for the Northern army at Yorktown; but, after all, they are merely a consequence of that beautiful system of slavery which the South is seeking to perpetuate. These assassin-like measures of the rebels are slowly but surely driving the North to exasperation. Another effect is also produced—one which will have a great result upon the determination of this contest and future reconstruction. There are tens of thousands of men in the Northern armies—indeed, I might say half the volunteers—who gave their services to the Government under the impression that the war would merely restore the former condition of affairs: these, officers and privates alike, have hitherto grumbled at the emancipationist policy inaugurated by the Government, and continually denied that the rebellion had anything to do with slavery. I conversed this morning with a brigade surgeon from New Jersey, who was one of this class, and I discovered, somewhat to my astonishment, that his opinions had undergone an entire change in consequence of these atrocities. The staffs of different generals afford good indications of the current of opinion among the Democratic element of the army, and satisfactorily prove to my mind that the whole North is coming round to the opinion of the party now in power, that the war cannot end without the annihilation of slavery.

Professor Lowe is on here with his balloons. An ascent was made this evening to a height of 950 feet, and the acting adjutant-general of Franklin's division was enabled to distinguish clearly the camp fires of the retreating enemy at fifteen miles' distance The New Jersey brigade has removed its encampment to the skirts of the woods where the battle took place yesterday, and we now lie on the road leading to the little town called Eltham, near the banks of the Pamunkey River. We are all in expectation of quitting this vicinity on the morrow, and reaching the enemy by forced marches—in which case I trust it will be rather cooler weather than we have enjoyed (?) to-day.

May 9.

Thirty thousand troops marched by my tent this afternoon between the hours of twelve and five. They took the road to Eltham, and I therefrom judge it is McClellan's intention to transport a considerable portion of his army across the Pamunkey River to the promontory between that stream and the Mattapony. He would thus be enabled to avail himself of the railroad between West Point and Richmond—no inconsiderable assistance to him should he require heavy siege artillery to attack the latter place. There is thought to be some appearance of a design on the part of the rebels to make their next stand for the possession of Richmond close to that city ; and perhaps they think McClellan cannot get up his heavy artillery from Yorktown to their capital under two or three weeks, at which period the hot weather will have set in, and the Northern troops will find it too hot to fight. A

considerable portion of this army—how large I know not—
is pushing along the road running parallel to the Pamunkey,
Major-General Stoneman and the cavalry being this afternoon five miles further on towards the point of attack than
we at this place. McClellan himself, I learn, is still at
Williamsburg, a few miles from Yorktown, near the James
River,—perhaps he is there superintending the passage of
troops to the southern bank of that stream; but why he
keeps constantly in the rear we cannot surmise satisfactorily. The iron-clad battery 'Galena' has ascended
the river, leaving the 'Monitor' to watch the 'Merrimac;'
and this certainly looks as though some such movement
as that above indicated were intended. A junction with
Burnside and a rapid advance upon Petersburg would cut
off Norfolk from reinforcements, and hem in the main
army of the Confederates upon their new line of the
Chickahominy.

We have received no mail since our arrival at this place,
and I am therefore unacquainted with passing events in
other sections of the country. Whatever is doing elsewhere is merely secondary in importance—auxiliary, in
fact—to the operations of the army on the Pamunkey
River. We have here the three best divisions of McClellan's command: the celebrated regiment, Berdan's sharpshooters, arrived this afternoon, and I understand that the
regulars and the artillery of reserve will be here tomorrow. With the James River held by Goldsborough's
fleet, the enemy cannot possibly get away from the vicinity
of Richmond; and this army, in conjunction with the
forces of Banks, M'Dowell, and Fremont, will strike a
blow which will annihilate the rebellion.

The negroes are coming into our lines in droves, and
affording invaluable assistance to our generals by their

knowledge of the country and the position of the enemy's forces. They march into the camps with the most charming confidence in the friendship of the Yankees, whom their masters represented to them as tyrants and negrohaters, and the information they possess is given without any need of questioning. We learn from them that the enemy's loss in the late engagement amounted to several hundreds in killed and wounded, mostly caused by the firing from our field-batteries and gunboats. They had two divisions engaged, among them some of the crack Southern regiments, as the Hampton Legion of South Carolina, the Texan Rangers, and the flower of the Alabama troops. Had they been able to bring artillery through the woods, our single division might have been driven into the river; they at all events prevented our executing a flank movement upon the retreating army from Yorktown, and enabled it to reach the Chickahominy without danger from us.

CHAPTER XI.

THE MARCH UP THE PENINSULA.

ELTHAM, VIRGINIA: May 10.

THIS little place, on the banks of the Pamunkey River, is now the head-quarters of Franklin's and Sedgwick's divisions, and in fact the base of operations of that portion of McClellan's immediate command which is advancing upon Richmond by way of York River. The Pamunkey is in reality the York River, and although scarcely indicated on the map, its breadth at Eltham is that of the Thames at Vauxhall. The town itself is scarcely worthy the name, being merely a half-dozen houses on the road leading through the woods to Richmond; but it offers advantages over the landing at the head of York River in consequence of possessing much deeper water and greater proximity to the city. The difficulties of the army are now really commencing, for everything depends upon the question of supplies—that is to say, transportation—and the roads here are execrable and very few in number. All the provisions and ammunition of this army, which probably exceeds 150,000 men, have to be brought from the Northern States to Baltimore, then shipped mainly on schooners, and towed down the Chesapeake Bay and up York River—a distance of 300 miles by water alone. The Chesapeake is occasionally a very tempestuous inland sea, and we are thus dependent on the winds and waves for all our supplies. Soon we shall have greater facilities, for the James River is now said to be opening up to us, and we shall thus be in a position to obtain what we require through numerous channels.

General FitzJohn Porter's division is still at the point where we landed originally, which, for want of a name, I called West Point. He cannot move forward until the two divisions at Eltham leave for the interior, all the open ground here being occupied by troops. I was down at the general's quarters this afternoon, and paid a visit to the camp of Berdan's Sharpshooters. The tents are by no means so picturesque as before Yorktown, but the men look forward to digging their rifle-pits within a week or two in sight of Richmond itself. Colonel Berdan was in high glee at the addition to his regiment of a new company, just arrived from Minnesota, and he spoke with much admiration of the qualities of these Western backwoodsmen. I find that only two of the companies are armed with the heavy 'target' or Swiss rifle, the others being generally provided with Sharpe's breech-loader, mounted with telescopic and globe sights. It is rather strange that whilst Americans are thoroughly decided against breech-loading cannon, all their inventors should be giving their attention to breech-loading muskets. There are Sharpe's, Burnside's, Maynard's, Colt's, and others whose names I forget.

May 12.

I cannot tell where to date from now, as we are in a place without a name and in the neighbourhood of nowhere else. We marched yesterday morning from Eltham, and, after turning numerous corners in the woods, finally debouched into a splendid open country at three miles' distance. Franklin's division is within eight miles of Kent

County Court-house, and we leave to-morrow morning at daybreak for the latter place, where McClellan's advance through the centre of the peninsula has already arrived.

I have gained much valuable information this morning, relative to the events of the past twelve months in the State of Virginia, from an old widowed lady, whose farm is within a stone's throw of our camp. Generals Franklin, Slocum, and Newton, and many of the principal officers of this division, have paid her visits since our arrival; and her house has, in fact, been a shrine which all have gladly approached. Mrs. Jennings, for such is the lady's name, in addition to being an out-and-out 'Union' woman, possesses great wit and sarcasm, and a pleasant volubility of the most attractive kind. Such women as she made Virginia 'the mother of Presidents;' but under the deteriorating influence of slavery, the race was becoming rapidly extinct. Her two eldest sons have been snatched from her, and forced to enter the rebel army; and she informs us that not a man nor boy is left 'to cultivate the ground who was capable of bearing arms. It became a question of field-labour or absolute starvation, and she, her daughters, and younger sons forthwith addressed themselves to the cultivation of the ground, raising barely sufficient for their own support. For many months past, she says, they have been compelled to use meal for coffee: sugar was at half a dollar in specie a pound, and all articles of clothing could only be obtained at ruinous prices. The dress she had on was woven by her own hands in a loom, out of cotton raised on her own farm, and I was surprised to hear that most Virginian families cultivate sufficient of the staple for home consumption. The old lady was born in the year 1800, and she told me she recollects well the war of 1812, and the marching of troops in front of her father's house. From her, as well as from other residents in the neighbourhood, I learn that agriculture is no longer attended to in this section of the State; neither corn nor wheat has been planted, and as the inhabitants are mostly poor, starvation is staring them in the face. With one solitary exception, a farmer who is known to have had intimate relations with the rebel leaders, all the inhabitants receive the Union army as a deliverer, and Mrs. Jennings assures us that when we reach Richmond we shall be astonished at the number of loyal persons in that city.

The head-quarters of the army which attacked our division last Wednesday were close to this lady's house, and she heard from Confederate officers that their number on that occasion was 30,000. The distance from her farm to York River was two and a half miles in a straight line, and the shells from the gunboats passed over her residence and burst far beyond. All the troops were not engaged, and when the enemy retreated towards evening they represented to the farmers in the vicinity that they were about taking up a new position near to Kent Court-house. We are now holding that place, with an entire division some miles beyond; and, if I am well informed, our advance pickets are within sixteeen miles of Richmond.

CUMBERLAND, VIRGINIA: May 13.

This place, now the head-quarters of General McClellan, is situated on the right bank of the Pamunkey River, two miles from Kent-County Court-house, and about twenty-five from Richmond. Like most of the Southern towns, it is nought but a collection of half-a-dozen houses; but the approaches are important, and the landing excellent; vessels drawing fifteen feet can ascend the stream above Cumberland, a distance of nearly 100 miles from Yorktown by water, and nine feet depth is found within a yard or two of the banks. The shores on either side are precipitous and covered with dense forests, and I have seldom seen a river more tortuous in its windings or so sylvan in beauty. We have here a considerable fleet of schooners and light draft vessels laden with provisions and forage for this immense army; and there are four gunboats, mounting 9, 10, and 11-inch guns, which have cleared the river of obstructions as far as White House, seven miles up stream. The master of one of the steamers tells me that in running from Cumberland to Eltham, where the Pamunkey flows into York River, he has to steer by every point of the compass, so serpentine are the windings; but the stream is broad and deep, and the current not too rapid. You will remark that McClellan is availing himself of these numerous streams, in which the Southern States are so rich, to bring supplies to his army, and I doubt much whether he will ever require to carry army stores over land a greater distance than from five to ten miles. It is necessary to examine a map on a very large scale before you can see half these rivers marked down, and most of those which appear but to be unimportant streamlets are really of considerable magnitude: the Pamunkey, forty miles from its mouth, and seventy-five from Too's Point, where the York River empties into the Chesapeake, is as large and much deeper than the Thames at Battersea.

I marched with the 4th New Jersey Regiment this morning, bringing up the rear of Franklin's division. Reveillée sounded at 4.30 A.M., and we commenced our journey at six o'clock. Next before us was the 95th Pennsylvania, following on the steps of the 31st, 32nd, and 16th New York, 5th Maine, 18th New York, 96th Pennsylvania, and so we marched until the latter came up to the 3rd New Jersey, which finally fell in as rear guard with ourselves. The wagon train belonging to each followed its regiment, and we were, therefore, an escort to it; a very necessary arrangement, seeing that we were entering the enemy's country, and within a few miles of the main Confederate army. The distance to be traversed was only twelve miles, but eight hours were barely sufficient to reach our destination, owing to the continual stoppages of the wagons: add to this a blazing sun and dusty roads, and it is easy to understand that the march was not entirely agreeable. The scenery, however, was most beautiful, hills and valleys, numerous watercourses, and occasional farm-houses dotting the landscape. Only a very small proportion of the ground is cleared, and that which heretofore was cultivated now mostly lies untilled. The entire male population is in the ranks of the Confederate army, and the negroes have been driven off to work on fortifications.

General McClellan passed along the road about eight A.M.; and we soon learned that the major portion of his army was in front of us, and marching towards Cumberland. At every cross road there would be a halt in order to allow the passage of teams belonging to other regiments, brigades, and divisions. Some idea may be formed of this immense chain of vehicles when I state that the general's private train numbers no less than twenty-eight wagons. What he wants with such a number I do not profess to state; but I hear many of his general officers complaining of the delay that this 'private train' causes. I hope to be able to give you in this letter the precise numbers of all the *matériel* brought by this army from the North.

We arrived at Kent Court-house about two o'clock, and

were met by a mounted officer, who informed us that our cavalry pickets had been driven in, and the enemy were coming down upon us in force. General McClellan and all the army but our two New Jersey regiments had turned off by the road leading to Cumberland; but Colonel Simpson of the 4th, being senior officer, immediately formed the Jersey troops into line of battle, and threw out skirmishers towards the foe. A dragoon shortly after came in from the front, and informed him that a masked battery had been opened upon our cavalry at five miles from the village, and the wagon trains were then ordered to proceed in all haste by the side road leading to Cumberland. The 14th Regulars and the New York Zouaves now came to our support at double quick, and, much to our surprise, they were followed by the 12th, 11th, 10th, 6th, 4th, 5th, 3rd, 2nd, and 8th Regulars, and a squadron of the Lincoln cavalry. Where they all came from we could not imagine, but this force of 10,000 men put our minds completely at ease for the safety of our baggage train. Believing that we were on the eve of a general engagement, I hastened with all speed to Cumberland, a distance of two miles, and arrived in time to see McClellan ride out with all his staff, a very regiment in numbers, in the direction of the point of attack. Three brigades were drawn up in line of battle on the brow of a hill, while the artillery harnessed up and awaited the order to advance. The enemy, after all, failed to show themselves; but the alarm proved satisfactorily that the army was ready for any contingencies. The troops had been marching all day in a hot sun; they were foot-sore, parched, and hungry; and yet they displayed most commendable alacrity in preparing to meet the foe. I feel satisfied they may be depended on for any service required of them, even though a summer's campaign in the Gulf States should become a necessity. This, however, I do not believe; for there is every prospect of destroying the entire Confederate army before it crosses the James River.

Heintzelman's *corps d'armée* is advancing up the peninsula with rapid strides, and Sumner's is to-day at Eltham; to-morrow it will be here, making an addition to our force of 35,000 men. Our camping-ground is situated in an immense amphitheatre surrounded by hills, except that portion which is bounded by the Pamunkey. This level valley is now covered with the tents of 60,000 men, and the scene is truly inspiring with the music of the bands, the countless camp-fires, and the loud neighings of so many thousand horses and mules. We hear a rumour that the entire army will press forward without delay after the enemy, for the droves of negroes coming into our lines assert that the Confederates are now evacuating Richmond, and seeking to reach Petersburg, south of the James River.

May 14.

Two divisions left here to-day for some point further on, and it was intended to move the entire army at this place to White House, where the railroad crosses the Pamunkey River; for some reason or other the movement was but partially carried out, but we all follow to-morrow, Franklin's division leading the advance. General Stoneman is already at White House, seven miles from here, with the vanguard of the army.

I have heard that to-day which leads me to believe the rebel army is preparing to make a final and desperate struggle at Richmond. The careful preparations of General M°Clellan and his cautious advance are certainly confirmatory of this opinion, added to which intrenching tools in enormous quantities are being carried along in the transports and by the troops. I should not be surprised to see a lengthy siege of the Confederate capital, carrying us forward into the summer months: the fall of Norfolk gives them a considerable addition to their force on the peninsula, and Jackson's and Smith's will greatly increase it also. There are no fears, however, for the result: McClellan's army alone has twelve divisions and fifty-eight batteries of field artillery; and the corps of Banks, Fremont, and M'Dowell are rapidly advancing from Northern Virginia to reinforce it. Meanwhile, the gunboats will not be idle in the James River, now that the 'Merrimac' is no longer a terror to them.

At White House we shall only be some twenty miles' distance from Richmond, and it is scarcely probable that the enemy will permit us to proceed further without hazarding an engagement. The longer this is postponed, the better for the North, for time will thus be given for the Union armies to surround the Confederates and cut off their retreat southwards. The antagonists are too close to each other to admit of much further delay.

CHAPTER XII.

BATTLE OF WILLIAMSBURG.

From an officer on the staff of Brigadier-General Kearny I have to-day heard particulars of the battle at Williamsburg. Brigadier-General Hooker, commanding the sister division in Heintzelman's *corps,* was the first to come up with the rear-guard of the Confederates at the town of Williamsburg. He attacked the enemy with fury, when the latter, discovering how small a force they had to deal with, returned in almost overwhelming numbers and well-nigh crushed him. Within two miles of the scene of action was the whole of Sumner's *corps d'armée;* but not having received orders to advance to Hooker's assistance, no command was given to march. 'Where is McClellan?' everybody asked and nobody could tell; and thus one of the finest divisions in the army was nearly sacrificed by the absence of the very man responsible for its safety. Between four and five o'clock in the afternoon Kearny came up at the head of his division; with a deafening cheer the troops followed their gallant chief into the thick of the *melée,* and the day was won. When all was over, the rebel army just commencing its retreat from the field, McClellan makes his appearance. Had he been present at the beginning of the engagement, there is every probability that the retreating Confederates would only have entered Richmond a disorganised rabble, for Hooker *single-handed* had kept them at bay since five o'clock in the morning, and Sumner with 30,000 men was close by without offering to render the slightest assistance.*

* Brigadier-General Hooker says, in his official report of the engagement: 'History will not be believed when it is told that the noble officers and men of my division were permitted to carry on this unequal struggle from morning until night, unaided, in the presence of more than 30,000 of their comrades with arms in their hands. Nevertheless it is true.'

So little was General McClellan acquainted with the details of the engagement at Williamsburg, that he absolutely ignored the services of the very officer who, at the close of the day, turned what threatened to become a disastrous defeat into a complete Union victory. In his despatch to the Secretary of War from Williamsburg on May 6, he states: 'The effect of *Hancock's* brilliant engagement yesterday was to turn the left of the enemy's line of works. He was strongly reinforced (McClellan does not say by whom), and the enemy abandoned the entire position during the night, leaving all his sick and wounded in our hands.' Not a single word for Kearny and his *division*; the whole credit for Hancock and his *brigade* alone. General Hooker states in his report: 'Between four and five o'clock General Kearny, with all his characteristic gallantry, arrived on the ground at the head of his division, and after having secured their positions, my division was withdrawn from the conflict, and held as a reserve until dark, when the battle ended, after a prolonged and severe conflict against three times my number, directed by the most accomplished general of the rebel army, Major-General J. E. Johnstone, assisted by Generals Longstreet, Pryor, Gohlson, and Pickett, with commands selected from the best troops in their army.'

Was this ignoring of the true state of the case intentional on the part of McClellan? It certainly was believed to be so in the *corps d'armée* of General Heintzelman. Kearny immediately complained of the injustice done to his troops, and McClellan was humiliated before the whole country.

CHAPTER XIII.

WHITE HOUSE.

WHITE HOUSE, PAMUNKEY RIVER, VIRGINIA :
May 17.

FRANKLIN'S late division reached this place on Thursday, and the main advance of the Grand Army is now within twenty-two miles of the rebel capital. Major-General Stoneman, with two regiments of infantry, two of cavalry, and a battery of six field pieces, is some miles in front of us, frequently skirmishing with the rear-guard of the enemy, and following them up towards the line of the Chickahominy. Our march from Cumberland, whence I last wrote you, was trying in the extreme, owing to the frightful condition of the roads. Although but five miles intervene between the two points, the entire day was consumed in the journey, and the troops arrived here knocked up, and had to camp it in a pouring rain on what was little better than a marsh. At no season of the year is this section of Virginia favourable to field operations, for when it ceases to rain the sky pours down an almost tropical heat. The alluvial is apparently bottomless, no 'hard' underlying the surface, and a ramrod with scarcely any pressure goes downward to the very head. Roads through cuttings exemplify this to the best extent, for even then you find nothing but alluvial unmixed with stones. Well does Virginia deserve her name! Little has been done, comparatively, towards reclaiming the State from its original wilds, and the few roads, if such they be called, are merely so many channels which serve to drain the interminable woods. What would Virginia become, if farmed by men who believe in the dignity of labour, and possess the energy and enterprise of northern citizens? Perhaps the day is not far distant, and the State will then prove itself the richest in agricultural resources of any in the Union. This result, however, can never be brought about by the men who now own the land.

We got from under our blankets at Cumberland in time to breakfast at three o'clock in the morning, and the different regiments composing our division fell into line shortly after. A brigade of infantry led the van, followed by the artillery and the wagon and ammunition train. Smith's division had gone over the same route the previous day, and as the rain had been falling for thirty-six hours, you may imagine something of the difficulties experienced by those who followed. We would march for five or ten minutes at a time in loose order, arms at will, then halt while the pioneers cut down young trees to corduroy the swampy road for the wagons to pass over: this style of progression irritates and fatigues the men infinitely more than any amount of continuous or rapid marching; and having already experienced its effects upon my own temper and limbs during the journey from Eltham to Cumberland, I struck out independently for White House, and after two hours' walking, jumping, and sticking in the mud, arrived wet through at our destination.

At the present time, there are three divisions encamped on this ground, and the entire army is en route to join them. No spot in Virginia is more admirably adapted for the purposes of a depôt than White House, nor is any place better fitted for an encampment. The scenery is almost a facsimile of the country about Kew and Richmond, except that the banks of the Pamunkey are much higher and the river more serpentine than the Thames; but I am compelled to give the palm of sylvan beauty to the American stream, spite of early associations. The trees are magnificent: under them Washington and the fathers (and grandfathers) of the Republic 'walked and talked' when the 'Old Dominion' still confessed allegiance to 'Good King George;' and here, too, where I now am writing, Colonel Washington first saw the Widow Custis, and overstayed his leave under the enchantment of her bright eyes. White House is so named after the residence of the farmer owning the estate, a magnificent property covering 7,000 acres, and as well stocked with slaves and 'other' cattle as any in Virginia. Colonel Lee, son of the general-in-chief of the rebel army, is the agent, if not owner, of the plantation at the present time, the former proprietor, George Custis, having died five or six years ago. The Washingtons, Custises, and Lees are all relatives by marriage, and are among the wealthiest and most aristocratic of the 'first families of Virginia.' The George Custis referred to above lived to an advanced age, and inasmuch as the slave question had not yet assumed its present alarming proportions, he was held in great respect by all classes of his fellow-citizens. Following the example of Washington, he set his negroes free on his death-bed—prospectively. In pursuance of a proviso in his will, all the slaves will receive their freedom next October, and George Custis is therefore looked upon by many as a very liberal-minded slaveholder. Perhaps, however, his actions previous to his last illness are the best indications of his character, particularly as some people in these United States regard death-bed manumissions as nothing more nor less than cheating one's descendants—death-bed repentances, in fact. The negroes now here declare, with convincing unanimity, in answer to interrogatories, that he was always selling them to the dealers; and it is therefore probable that this beautiful estate, hallowed by so many ennobling recollections, has of late years been 'a nigger-raising farm'—a place to breed 'property' in, as others breed cattle or rabbits. An immense revolution is now working on the Northern mind through the army. In Upper Virginia, around Alexandria, and towards the Rappahannock, the farms are really what they purport to be, but, south of this river, agriculture is merely resorted to as forage for 'stock'—stock meaning slaves raised for the Southern market. In the marches of this army from the head of York River, through Eltham, Cumberland, and other villages, we have invariably found this to be the case; and whenever we came across any landowner who remained on his estate, he thought it sufficient excuse for the system in pleading that it was much more profitable than any other. Slaves are no longer restored by us to their masters, and what is still more, I can see or hear of no disposition on the part of most of the officers in the army to restore them: the 'institution' is cut up, root and branch, in the peninsula between the York and James Rivers; and wherever the Northern legions set foot, experience teaches the same unvarying lesson. It was so at Port Royal. Phelps was merely three months too hasty in Mississippi. Burnside has had to check the impetuosity of his followers in North Carolina, whilst we in Virginia are surpassing the rest. When we reached Cumberland a few days ago we, as usual, captured and confiscated a large amount of grain and forage belonging to the planter 'owning,' as they say here, 'thereabouts.' The individual in question sought out one of the principal officers of the staff, and asked him not to seize the corn, as he required it to feed his servants, meaning his slaves. 'Oh! you haven't got any servants now,' replied the officer, and the planter has since had leisure to reflect that, were it not for the rebellion of his State, his property would not have been confiscated. One United States' Quartermaster or Commissary is ten times more a practical abolitionist than a dozen theorists like Wendell Phillips and Lloyd Garrison.

I believe this anti-slavery feeling, this conviction that the Union can never be restored except on the ruins of the institution which has caused the rebellion, is shared in by most of this army. A prominent member of General McClellan's staff said to me three days ago: 'If this war were to end here, the slave power would regain its influence within a few years. We have, as yet, gained nothing but emancipation in the District of Columbia.' The inference from his remark is obvious; but I do not at all agree with him as to nothing much being gained. The whole Northern mind has undergone a change, and everything else must, of necessity, follow.

On his arrival here, General McClellan took up his quarters at the White House; but not desiring to deal harshly with so influential a family as the Lees, he has since moved half a mile to the rear, and sentries are placed around the house to prevent anyone entering it. The soldiers grumble at this 'kid glove' deference to rebels. All his staff is with him, and the encampment covers several acres in extent, the position being considerably in advance of the army on the road to Richmond. The tents of our three divisions are pitched on a plain of some three or four hundred acres, bounded on one side by the romantic Pamunkey River, and surrounded elsewhere by a magnificent forest. This vast field is covered with thick clover in bloom, a foot high, and our thousands of horses are having a good time of it generally.

White House is to be made the basis of our operations against Richmond, and it is now being turned into an immense depôt. The river is absolutely filled with shipping, vessels drawing twelve feet of water ascending hither without difficulty. Several gunboats of 500 tons burden, sister-craft to the 'Seneca,' 'Unadilla,' &c., which rendered so much service at Port Royal, lie off in the stream, and, were it not for the ruins of the railroad bridge, they could run still higher. Canal barges, placed side by side, form efficient docks, the sides of the river are covered with unending commissary and ordnance stores, and the ever-present Sanitary Commission is erecting its depôts and unloading its vessels of their welcome stores. We have telegraphic communication with West Point, and, I believe, down the peninsula to Fortress Monroe; for so fast as the army advances, the signal corps run the wires from tree to tree. The post-office is well managed under military authority. We have postal communication daily with the North, and receive letters thence with equal regularity. Regimental mails are made up in the evening, delivered to division head-quarters at night, forwarded to General McClellan's camp at sunrise next morning, and despatched to Fortress Monroe by steamer about eight o'clock. The mail leaves the latter place for Baltimore at five o'clock in the afternoon, reaching the Maryland metropolis next day, when the railroads take it up and distribute it through the Northern cities. This letter will leave White House early on Monday morning, and reach

New York late on Tuesday night; were the Wednesday's steamer for Europe starting from Boston I should have to post my letter a day earlier. I am given to understand these postal arrangements will be continued with equal regularity throughout the campaign, and it is a common remark amongst the officers and men that they now obtain their letters much more rapidly than when the army was on the banks of the Potomac.

May 18.

Sunday has, indeed, been a day of rest with this army. In pursuance of orders from head-quarters, divine service was held in all the regiments here encamped, and, I learn, throughout the entire Federal army on this peninsula. The morning was hot and close, and at the hour of service, half-past ten, the heat was almost too great for ordinary troops to withstand it. At the same hour the bands of the different regiments gave the signal for all to fall into line; the men were paraded for a few minutes, then formed into hollow squares, face inwards, and the chaplains prayed and addressed them during half-an-hour. I have never seen so much decorum exhibited by any men as was shown by these troops. I scarcely observed one who was not uncovered, although on account of the sun no order was given to that effect. The chaplain of the regiment with which I have taken up my quarters gave notice at the close that a prayer-meeting would be held in his camp at 7 o'clock in the evening, and one-quarter of the regiment took part voluntarily in the proceedings, closing with the Doxology, which sounded well in the silent evening air.

When the sun was at its hottest, I rambled inquisitively through the interminable lines of tents, and watched the thousands of blue-coated soldiers of the Republic rolling in the rich clover beneath the shade of canvas, and a considerable number reading tracts to their comrades, or silently. These they had received from their chaplains; 'Cromwell's Soldiers' Bible' being very popular with all. I could not but draw most favourable conclusions as to the future of these bones and sinews of the Free North, who look upon religion as a reality, and no mere form or ceremony. Wherever I travel in this country it is the same unvarying story—an absolute absence of that infidelity which seems to have swallowed up the higher classes of European society. Rich and poor alike, men in office and out of it, officers of the regular and volunteer services, all evince respect for sacred things. Swearing of course abounds here to an immense extent, but no one professes, as elsewhere in the 'civilised world,' an ignoring or denial of religion. Throughout the free States the churches are filled with attentive worshippers, the males predominating; doctrinal distinctions are toned down, and all sects work together harmoniously towards a common end. Faith is the national characteristic of this people—faith in God and themselves; and history teaches a lie if such faith have not been the motto of all nations who have risen to supremacy in this world.

An European roaming through these interminable rows of tents, listening to the conversation of soldiers from every nation under heaven (I will say Europe, to avoid the charge of exaggeration), cannot but remark the absence of those 'trooper' songs and talk so characteristic of European armies. The influence of the 'dominant race' is so marked, that with the exception of certain adjectives and emphasis obnoxious to the cloth on other than merely grammatical grounds, there is a total absence of vicious songs and conversation. The Americans, as a race, are readers and thinkers *par excellence*; and, as soldiers, they are perfect cormorants for all kinds of literature, especially newspapers. The songs in camp are those harmonious sentimental negro melodies, national hymns, and the favourite of all, grand old 'John Brown.' But it must not be supposed that fun is absent either among those 'to the manor born' or naturalised citizens. Strolling through the camps yesterday, I overhead a smart discussion about duty and glory, when a Teuton volunteer gave his opinion of the latter in this wise:—'Mein Gott, vat is glory? Glory is ven you are shot in den belly mit a Minié ball, and you no like him tree days. Den you roll youself up in der Shtripes and der Shtars, and you die like ein leetle dog. And you sees your name shpelt wrong in der papers next morning. Mein Gott, dat is glory!' I thought a worse definition might be given of the 'bubble reputation.'

11 o'clock p.m.

Our division moves forward towards Richmond tomorrow morning at four o'clock, followed by the remainder of the army here encamped, and General McClellan with his entire staff leaves at seven. I am informed that our day's march will place us seven miles nearer the rebel capital, and I therefore judge we shall sleep to-morrow night on the banks of the Chickahominy. The other divisions in the peninsula are moving rapidly towards that stream, and the pickets of the two contending armies will probably be in sight of each other within the next forty-eight hours.

The Confederates are making a similar stand here to that under Beauregard at Corinth, and in both cases out of reach of the gun-boats, which they so much fear. Halleck's inaction may perhaps appear strange, but the reason will soon be accounted for; probably, too, during the coming week. Generals Sigel and Curtis, the victors of Pea Ridge, in Arkansas, have been lost sight of for some time. Their armies now turn up 200 miles south-east of the Ridge, and within two days' junction with General Steel's division at Jacksonport, sixty miles only from the Mississippi. Here a fleet is waiting to transport them across the river, and they will then be in a position to execute a flank movement with 40,000 men upon Beauregard at Corinth.

BOSHER'S PLANTATION (20 miles from Richmond),
VIRGINIA: May 19.

The Sixth Army Corps, commanded by General Franklin, left White House this morning at five o'clock, and simultaneously with it, FitzJohn Porter's *corps d'armée*, the Fifth, started from this point by a different road. Franklin's present command is composed of his old division and that of Smith; Porter's consist of his former brigades, with the addition of the Regulars under Sykes. I should estimate the two corps at 30,000 men each, and they are certainly made up of the most disciplined and reliable troops in the grand army. FitzJohn Porter and Franklin are bosom friends of McClellan, who has long endeavoured to make them the equals in rank of officers much their seniors. At the period of the last organisation of the Army of the Potomac, they were nominated by the General-in-chief as *corps* commanders; but Congress failing to see any other motive for such advancement than a personal one, flatly refused its endorsement. McClellan has now the opportunity to do as he pleases without regard to parliamentary objectors; and although he cannot give increased rank or pay, he can award what commands he may choose. Franklin I have long known, as a quiet amiable gentleman, but slow and apathetic as a soldier. He will prove a good officer to fall back upon in case of emergency, and I believe his errors will all be on the side of over-caution—the great failing of this army under its present leaders. FitzJohn Porter has many more enemies than friends, due in great measure, doubtless, to the unfair partiality shown him by McClellan. When the army was in the trenches before Yorktown, Porter's troops had little duty to perform, while other commands were constantly overworked; and when General Hamilton, commanding the second division in Heintzelman's *corps*, had sufficient manliness to complain of this partiality, he was immediately dismissed, and Kearny placed at the head of his division. Porter is the opposite of Franklin in manner, being cold, uncordial, and intensely autocratic. He would make a capital Hetman of Cossacks.

Leaving White House, ere the sun had doffed his grey morning robe, we marched backwards from the Pamunkey River, and followed the road leading to Tunstall's, so named after the landed proprietor. It would seem as though the scenery of this State would become more and more beautiful the further we progress towards Richmond, and certainly nothing that I have yet seen of Virginia at all equals the scenery of this day's march. A mile from McClellan's camp we passed the residence of Dr. Meakin, a wealthy planter who opposed secession at the outset, but confesses to a change in opinions since the actual outbreak of hostilities. Many officers of our army have visited him and his family during our stay at White House, and, while admitting his sympathy with his own section, he asserts that the North must be successful, as it can show five soldiers to one of the Confederates. This gentleman is nearly the sole resident of these parts remaining in the district, the others having fled at our approach, or, which is more probable, being now in the ranks of Johnston's army. Leaving this plantation, the road skirted woods bright with the beauties of young spring; on our right the country stretched far away in an undulating plain, dotted here and there with well-kept plantations, and reminding one strongly of a peaceful English landscape. Two miles brought us to the Richmond and York River Railroad, where we found several companies of a New York regiment engaged in rebuilding a bridge over a stream, and the remains of the camps of General Stoneman's cavalry advance. The scenery now became finer than before, and I can only compare it to our Southern Downs, with the luxuriant foliage of Windsor in the hollows. Occasionally the roads would be arched with varied-coloured trees for a distance of several hundred yards, and on emerging from the cover we would catch sight of hills rising one above the other, and the long lines of many thousand bayonets flashing diamond-like on their crests. So lovely was everything around, and so perfumed the morning air, that many of the troops regretted their march did not extend five miles further towards Richmond.

Bosher's Plantation is to-day the head-quarters of the grand army, McClellan being here with all his staff, and Franklin's and Porter's corps camping around him. You will not find the place marked on any map, and I can only explain its position by stating that it is some seven miles from White House, twenty from Richmond, three from the Chickahominy, and three-quarters of a mile from the Pamunkey. We are still near the gunboats, and much of our supplies may still reach us by way of the river. A few days, however, will see the railroad again in working order, the enemy having retreated so rapidly as to leave the route intact, with the exception of the bridges.

Our march, you will observe, is parallel to the Pamunkey, and not as yet direct upon Richmond. This is in order to avoid the swampy region of country traversed by the Chickahominy. We are, in fact, advancing upon the Confederate capital by the hilly ridge forming the backbone of the Peninsula, the country north of us draining itself into the Pamunkey, or Upper York River, while the streams flowing southwards empty themselves into the marshes of the Chickahominy. The entire region, however, is far too thickly wooded for us to see far in advance; but Stoneman, with his numerous scouts, is ahead some five miles, and keeps the General-in-Chief *au courant* of the enemy's movements. But few of Johnston's men have yet been seen, and the impression prevails in camp that the rebel commanders are looking for us on the chosen line of the Chickahominy. Maybe we shall receive news of their presence to-morrow on the banks of the Pamunkey, but in any case we are prepared for them, as the whole of McClellan's army is within a few hours' march of this position.

LIPSCOMBE'S PLANTATION (18 miles from Richmond): May 20.

Leaving Bosher's at three o'clock this afternoon, our division marched five miles, and camped at the above place two hours after. Our course was not directly towards Richmond, the intention being to reach the cross roads in the lower corner of Hanover county, whence the route is straight for the capital. As we progressed in our march the country gradually opened— forests became the exception, not the rule—and but for the absence of hedges, I might have fancied myself in peaceful England. Farmhouses, with their numerous out-buildings, sprinkled the landscape more frequently, and all had white flags flying on the gates or gables, begging from us neutrality. My own researches, as also those of officers with whom I have since conversed, satisfied me that the universal feeling in this section of the State is hostile to the Federal government; but the planters hide their opinions, and receive the advancing army with ominous silence. Some of the residents were sitting out in their gardens with their families, watching the passing regiments, whilst, in one or two cases, the families had left their homes, and nought but empty buildings remained.

During the whole of our march we heard heavy firing on our left, and, judging from the direction and distance, we put it down to the gunboats on the James River.

M'Dowell is understood to be on his way to join us from Fredericksburg, coming across Hanover county. What Banks is doing nobody here pretends to explain; judging from what little information we possess, he has lately been compelled to retreat, but matters connected with other commands are kept so quiet that it would be dangerous to draw any conclusion whatever from his movements.

We passed General McClellan during the march; he had been to Bottom Bridge, on the Chickahominy, and was returning in company with general Franklin, the Count of Paris, and others. We hear that the division of our army, under General Couch, is at Bottom Bridge, the road there crossing the river and passing through a swamp seven miles in circumference, towards Richmond. Here is the direct route for us to the rebel capital, and the one by which it is understood the Confederates expect to meet us; the road we are taking, though circuitous, is much more practicable for our immense parks of artillery and the wagon train. General Van Vliet, the quarter-master of the army under McClellan's command in the Peninsula, informs me there are upwards of 5,000 wagons and ambulances (many of them drawn by six horses) under his immediate orders. This movement upon Bottom Bridge is probably nought but a feint to engage the attention of the enemy while we turn their left flank to the northward. Meanwhile we know very little of the whereabouts of the rest of our army except our own and Couch's, Smith's, and Porter's divisions, four only out of the twelve. We hear, however, that they are advancing towards Richmond by roads to the southward, their march being much more direct than the circuitous route of Franklin's and Porter's corps; the two latter are under the immediate eye of the General-in-Chief, his camp always accompanying them, and they are evidently intended to act as the reserve.

COLD HARBOUR (11 MILES FROM RICHMOND), May 22.

We marched seven miles yesterday in the hottest part of the day, and arrived at Cold Harbour between four and five in the afternoon, after ten hours' perspiration. Our brigade brought up the rear, instead of being in the advance as on the day previous, and we had to wait continually for those before us to move on, the artillery much delaying us, owing to the badness of the roads in the hollows between the hills. The march told greatly upon the men, and I am not at all surprised to hear this morning that nearly sixty are under the surgeon's care from so long exposure to the sun. The wagons of our division did not arrive until late at night, and while the troops slept under the shelter tents (*tentes d'abri*), which are carried on the knapsacks, the officers rolled themselves in their blankets, and rested with the starlit canopy of heaven above them I had some difficulty at first in 'steeping my senses in forgetfulness,' owing to the energetic attacks of ticks, nits, beetles, bugs, spiders, mosquitoes, &c., with which Virginia swarms, and still more the fear of snakes (two had already been killed by one man since our arrival); but exhaustion finally got the better of me, and I slept refreshing slumbers, with a mild southern wind blowing over me. I awoke this morning at *réveillée*, with my hair and blankets saturated with dew.

Before leaving yesterday's camping ground, I had a conversation with 'a very intelligent contraband,' as the slaves are now generally called. He is lately from Richmond, where he 'belongs,' and had previously given information to General McClellan of much importance. He states that three weeks ago the authorities of that city caused all the tobacco in the vast storehouses there to be hauled into a field at some distance and burnt. Jefferson Davis, about the same period, removed his family southwards, and the impression prevailed universally that Richmond was considered no longer tenable by the Confederates. Last Sunday week the authorities went to the 'coloured' church, arrested all the congregation during service, and sent the males to sink vessels in the James River, and the females to attend the hospitals. Much grumbling was covertly given vent to by the poor negroes on account of their not being permitted to change their 'Sunday clothes,' bought by them out of months of hard economy. My informant is a man so nearly white, that in Europe nobody would suppose he possessed the slightest tint of African blood in his veins; and, though a slave, he has had the utmost confidence reposed in him by his master, buying and selling for him over a great portion of the State. He considers the rebel army at Richmond—that is to say, the entire command under Johnston—numbers some 125,000 men, basing his opinion upon what he has heard and his own knowledge. The force is mainly composed of Virginians and conscripts—many old, and all comparatively undrilled and undisciplined. He says they are preparing to make a stand five miles from the city; all the negroes for miles round are employed in throwing up earthworks, and large forts, built ten months ago, surround the capital. Generals Magruder, Floyd, and Wigfall, with 60,000 men, are on the road we are now following.

Cold Harbour is so named from the fact of an Indian having been frozen to death here at the time of the first settling of Virginia. The country around, like all we have marched through, is comparatively unplanted, verifying the assertion of Mrs. Jennings, near Eltham, that all the labouring population has been forced into the rebel army. The distance of Richmond by the road is eleven miles, but on foot or horseback, through the woods, it is only eight. I believe we rest here to-day, in order to permit the rest of our army to come up.

Cold Harbour : May 24.

There was no possibility of forwarding this letter in time for the steamer from New York, owing to the army being on the march. Our progress has been delayed the past few days in consequence of the state of the roads, but the waggons of our two *corps d'armée* have made two trips to White House since our arrival at this place, and we are now in a position to march upon Richmond. The rain has poured down incessantly during the last twenty-four hours, and our forward movement was countermanded in consequence; but we have just received orders (10 P.M.) to march to-morrow morning at 8 o'clock, our brigade heading the division.

By this evening McClellan's army will hold the left bank of the Chickahominy from the James River to the point where the Virginia Central Railroad crosses the former stream to the north of the rebel capital. The bridge there was destroyed by our troops the night before last, so as to prevent any movement of the Confederates under Jackson upon our right flank, and it is believed that our division will march to-morrow towards that point and cross the Chickahominy immediately after. This, however, is only a surmise, the utmost secrecy being maintained. We know, however, that Heintzelman's corps holds the left of our line, Keyes the centre, Porter and Franklin the right; and, arguing from the fact of McClellan's head-quarters being with the two latter, we judge that the main struggle will fall upon us. M'Dowell, it is again asserted, is on his way to join us from Fredericksburg, the order being given him to effect a junction with the army last Monday. The railroad from this point to the head of York River (West Point) is now complete, and trains will commence running on Monday next.

The enemy are in force the other side of the Chickahominy, and it is generally believed that we shall have to invest Richmond. Heavy siege guns are being brought to our front for that purpose.

CHAPTER XIV.

THE LINES OF THE CHICKAHOMINY.

ON THE BANKS OF THE CHICKAHOMINY
(SIX MILES FROM RICHMOND): May 26.

PORTER's and Franklin's *corps d'armée*, the right wing of McClellan's army, have now reached that point where a further advance must bring on a general engagement. The two divisions composing Franklin's command are encamped in an immense wheat-field, and close in their rear, acting as supports, are the troops under FitzJohn Porter. Approaching this our present position from our previous camping-ground at Cold Harbour, the land gradually rises towards the river, and our oceans of tents are therefore hidden from view of the enemy by the summit of the hills in our front. A belt of high trees covers the slope facing the foe, and we should be perfectly shielded from any notice were it not for the smoke of our fires by day and the reflection of the lights at night. The enemy must be well acquainted with the fact of our present position, but for some reason or other they have in no way molested us since our arrival; perhaps they are waiting for McClellan to assume the offensive, and, if so, they may have to wait for some days to come. I hear on very good authority that unless they attack us we shall not make any advance until General Wool occupies the city of Petersburg, and Fremont and Banks are within close proximity to Richmond, and M'Dowell has effected a junction with our right flank. Yet, according to the opinion of most here, we are certainly strong enough to tackle the foe without further assistance; else why has he so studiously kept out of our way since the fights at Williamsburg and West Point?

Major-General Wool, at last accounts, was within seven miles of Petersburg, at the head of 20,000 men. These numbers may be, and probably are, an exaggeration; but the enemy cannot have any considerable force at that point, as every available regiment has been drawn away for the defence of Richmond.

The tent in which I am now writing is pitched on the edge of the road leading through the woods to the Chickahominy. A hundred paces bring us to the base of a high hill, from the summit of which a magnificent view is obtained of the valley separating us from the enemy's position, and at a distance of a quarter of mile of open flows the river, varying in breadth from twenty to forty feet, and generally unfordable. Trees and bushes skirt our edge of the stream, affording admirable cover for our advanced pickets, and behind a copse at a distance of twelve hundred yards we occasionally catch sight of the enemy's cavalry videttes. The horizon is bounded by woods, judged by artillery officers to be a mile and a half from our hill, and midway between the thick groves of high trees and the videttes we have detached a battery. The ground occupied by the Confederates rises panorama-like in front of us, and as their position is considerably more elevated than our own, our encampment is altogether under fire of their guns. We expected to be shelled by them this morning, but both sides seem loth to begin.

General Stoneman, with two infantry regiments, two of

cavalry, and two batteries of flying artillery, is now occupying Mechanicsville, a village on the northern bank of the Chickahominy, two miles from this encampment. A deserter came into his quarters this morning, and reported a division in front of us composed of three Georgia brigades and a couple of field batteries. If this be the enemy's proportion of artillery to a division, we are double their strength in this arm of the service, without taking into account our artillery of reserve numbering twenty-two batteries. They also labour under another great disadvantage in the inferiority of their fuses; few of their shells burst, and they appear to use none other than those on the Boerman principle. Their practice also is generally poor, vastly below that of the Federal artillerists both in range and precision.

M'Dowell is represented to be at the head of 40,000 men. Banks and Fremont have some 35,000 between them, and Wool has, it is said, 20,000. When the great blow is struck, McClellan will not have much less than a quarter of a million troops under his immediate command, and the above additions to his present army will give him forty more field batteries at the lowest computation. We hear that the Confederates have 200,000 men in and around Richmond, but a large portion of these are conscripts, and many of them armed merely with pikes.

Orders from head-quarters lead us to expect an early engagement. For some days past the musicians of the different regiments have had an easy time of it, no music being permitted, and no calls by fife or drum. Fires also are extinguished at 6 P.M., so that no lurid glare in the heavens may point out our position to the enemy. Medical officers of the different *corps d'armée* are ordered to report every Sunday morning to Dr. Tripler, the chief of McClellan's medical staff, and their reports must give exact information upon the number of sick in the camp hospitals, and the prevailing complaints. Since the army left Yorktown we have had a constant increase of bowel complaints, diarrhœa, &c., from impurities in the water: at one camping ground we find the streams or springs impregnated with alum, at another the water collects in clay beds, and each stopping place gives us a liquid which no more resembles *aqua pura* than the decoction which flows between Westminster and London bridges. Add to this the 'bread,' as it is called officially, or 'hard tack,' its more familiar name, made certainly of pure wheaten flour, but baked hard as adamant: nobody with the slightest gastronomic 'proclivities' could ever attain a taste for this substance, although the men good-humouredly talk of going without their dinners in order to obtain sufficient appetite to enjoy it at tea; and one volunteer told a harder story to his comrades than the 'tack' itself, declaring that a shot during a skirmish had struck him in the region of the stomach, but a hearty meal of these crackers stopped the missile *instanter*. These biscuits are really indigestible, unless softened previous to eating; but men in the field have little time for culinary operations. Two or three days' fresh meat, following on a course of salt 'horse' (beef) or pork, will also induce diarrhœa; but perhaps this may be due to the rough manner in which the rations are cooked by the men themselves. Orders were given yesterday that henceforward no meat shall be broiled or fried; but it is too early to determine whether this will have the desired effect of checking the complaints.

I have mentioned in a previous letter that the general hospitals of the army are established at White House, the point on the Pamunkey River which we last quitted before pushing into the interior towards Richmond. As we progressed through the country to this our present encampment, the brigade and division surgeons have set their seals upon different houses and outbuildings, in the shape of small red flags, taking care, however, not to interfere with the owners who have chosen to remain. I understand the same course has been pursued on all the other roads by which this immense army is approaching Richmond, and the medical staff is being greatly increased daily by the arrival of volunteer surgeons from the different Northern States. And they will all be needed, if we are to have as determined a struggle in front of the rebel capital as at Williamsburg, Corinth, and Donelson.

General Order No. 128, issued yesterday, gives precise instructions to officers and troops relative to crossing the Chickahominy. The men are to be ready for action, in light marching order; knapsacks to be left with baggage train; three days' rations in havresacks; forty rounds of ammunition in cartridge boxes, and twenty additional in the pockets. Limber and caisson boxes must be packed to their utmost capacity; ammunition wagons to be held in readiness, but not to cross the river until so ordered, following the same rule as the baggage train which will be parked under the quarter-masters on our present camping ground. I hear that the entire army will be thrown across the Chickahominy at the same moment, and take up a position on the brow of the hills beyond the river, only the twenty-two batteries of reserve artillery remaining on this side for the purpose of shelling the enemy in the woods; such I am informed is the present plan, but it is not unlikely to be seriously modified by circumstances. In any case we shall have an up-hill fight for some three-quarters of a mile, struggling across the open, with batteries playing upon us from the woods.

May 27.

We have again passed a peaceable day, so far as our own division is concerned; but since noon until the shades of evening, we have heard cannonading and musketry in the distance. The sound came from a point almost due north of us, and we are unable to make out whether it arose from the advancing columns of McDowell, or from the *corps-d'armée* under FitzJohn Porter. The former is within easy distance of us, if we may credit what is stated in camp; he is reported to have signalled to us by means of rockets the night before last, but nobody ventures to express a decided opinion as to his exact whereabouts. From a conversation with one of McClellan's aids this forenoon, I judge he is not far from effecting a junction with us, but further information was withheld from me for the present. Maybe we are awaiting McDowell's arrival before attempting anything at this point.

FitzJohn Porter marched off this morning in a north-westerly direction, with the object of destroying a certain portion of the railroad between Richmond and Fredericksburg, so as to prevent the retreat of the army in front of McDowell upon the main body under Johnston. The firing above referred to may have proceeded from him, but in the opinion of many artillery officers the cannonading was much farther off. At first we heard it but faintly; after two hours' continuance it broke out apparently ten miles nearer this camp, and was subsequently renewed at the previous point, but much more distinctly. To-morrow we may learn where it actually transpired, but for the present we are compelled to content ourselves with mere surmises.

One brigade of this division, with Hexamer's field battery, marched this morning into Mechanicsville, two miles hence in a north-westerly direction, and about a thousand yards from the Chickahominy. A road runs in almost a mathematically straight line from this village to Richmond, the distance being less than five miles; the turnpike-road crosses the river by a bridge, which the enemy have partially destroyed, and before we can undertake any advance it must of necessity be repaired. As far as my walks have extended, and from all I gather from others, I establish the fact of Confederate pickets lining the opposite banks of the Chickahominy for miles on each side of us. Last night was peculiarly favourable for conjecturing the enemy's force, as the heavens were covered with rain clouds, reflecting the camp fires of an army which no one estimated at less than 150,000 men. There was a general impression, however, that many of the fires were built to deceive us; for a force so large as that represented by the reflection above might certainly have kept our army from approaching so close to Richmond. Men and officers ask each other, 'Are we being humbugged, or is Joe Johnston out-generalling McClellan?' Time will show. The lurid haze reminded me of the sky overhanging Manchester or Birmingham at night-time, and was not, I should judge, far removed from the trees bounding our horizon to the southward. Some officers here believe the enemy are playing a sharp game upon us by throwing up heavy batteries behind the woods in our front; and the more I see of the position across the river, the more I feel satisfied of the tremendous struggle now approaching. Yet we remain idle on this side the stream—no reconnaisances to obtain information of the enemy's strength and operations—no attempt on our part to cross the trumpery ditch.

From the woods, in which we catch an occasional glimpse of the enemy's pickets, to the banks of the debatable river in the valley, the land forms a perfect natural *glacis*, up which our men must advance for three quarters of a mile, exposed to the fire of batteries which all feel are being constructed behind the trees. The enemy, as yet, has given us no further proof of his existence than by his camp fires, and we on our part are strangely careful not to incur his hostility. Deserters and 'contrabands' inform us that Beauregard, lately recalled from Corinth, is now in command of the left wing of the rebel army covering Richmond. If this intelligence be correct, he is immediately opposed to us, and he certainly will not permit our crossing without doing everything in his power to prevent us. No position could be better chosen for the defence of any point than this line of the Chickahominy—a narrow but deep river lined with swamps on one bank, the shore on the other side rising rapidly for nearly a mile towards the woods, and affording no chance of cover to the advancing assailants. Still, there are many fords in the stream, whilst in some places an active man might leap from one bank to the other; in others, tall trees grow close to the water, as though placed there purposely to invite bridge-building; but our army lies perfectly idle, most of the officers silent and morose, the men grumbling.

Professor Lowe's balloons are up constantly. We have had two up in the sky this day, one towards Mechanicsville, the other in the vicinity of Bottom's Bridge, where the Richmond and York River railroad crosses the Chickahominy. The enemy evidently considers this ballooning a mean sort of way of prying into his private concerns; and, certainly, a man 1,000 feet in air has a more comprehensive view of things in general than he who reconnoitres off the back of a horse or roof of a house. But General McClellan confines himself to this one means of obtaining information; for I cannot learn, after the most diligent enquiry, that any other reconnaissances are taken than by these balloons. Now, the country hereabouts is one dense forest, covering lofty hills and deep valleys, with only here and there a patch of 'open': what benefit can accrue from ballooning I cannot imagine, unless high elevations enable a man to look through dense forests. We have a large cavalry force absolutely lying idle. General Stoneman, after driving the retreating rebels up the Peninsula in splendid style, is quietly encamped out of the way to the rear of Mechanicsville, he himself grumbling at having nothing to do; his officers asking why they have been brought to the Peninsula at all, while the privates are listless and disappointed. An officer of the 8th Illinois cavalry told me yesterday he supposed the horses would soon be cut up into army beef, and the men armed with the inevitable spade and set to digging. Now and then the balloons do some good. Yesterday, for instance, they informed us that a large force of the enemy was advancing upon the position of General Keyes, near Bottom's Bridge, and the order was immediately given to hold ourselves in readiness for an attack, and perchance a general engagement. The affair passed off without result, much to the disgust of the troops, who cannot understand our seeming delay. This forenoon, the enemy bombarded the balloon from beyond Mechanicsville, firing several rifled shot in close proximity to the men holding the cords; one of these struck an oak tree within fifty feet of the æronaut, and the balloon was forthwith removed to a safer distance.

From Mechanicsville, as also from some of the houses in

this vicinity, we obtain a view of the steeples of Richmond, but we are not sufficiently near to see the city itself. The country is beautiful in appearance, although fearfully unhealthy in this region; and wherever there is high ground and absence of trees and undergrowth, farm-houses and gentlemen's residences heighten the beauty of the landscape. I have been much surprised at the unvarying respect paid to property by the troops composing this army. Hedges are never seen in these latitudes,—the 'green lanes of England' stand alone in their matchless loveliness,—but boundaries are marked by pine timbers some ten feet long and four inches in width and thickness, roughly split with an axe, in fact. President Lincoln might describe the *modus operandi,* if he have not forgotten his first love. Ten or a dozen of these rails, supported at both ends at proper distances, make a very efficient obstacle to cattle and other 'insects,' as they call buffalo on the prairie'; and being well dried by exposure to the sun they are naturally sought after by the troops to build fires. When a regiment arrives on a new camping ground, so soon as the muskets are stacked and orders given to pitch tents, men will be seen running off by hundreds to bring these coveted rails from the fences; and it is a hard thing to be told, after a long and tedious march through the drenching rain and fathomless mud, not to touch this property of the rebels, but to cut down green wood from the forest. The men very properly say:—' We may be shot down by the rebels, blown to pieces on the march by their torpedoes, or murdered in cold blood by guerillas; we may shoot them in return, and, "under orders," seize their corn, flour and forage, but we must not touch their fences.' When approaching any new camping ground, sentries are placed on all the buildings in the neighbourhood, notwithstanding the almost invariable abuse showered on 'invaders' and 'd——d Yankees;' for this section of Virginia is Secessionist to the backbone, and firmly convinced that the army of the Potomac is to be annihilated in front of Richmond. It is a mystery from what source these orders come to the troops: the Government at Washington cannot be a party to them, and it certainly seems strange that a population so hostile is to be courted and cherished to the great detriment of the Union soldiers. The farmers in the South have the assurance to complain to the Federal officers of their hay, corn, and oats being 'stolen' from them, as they term it, although a receipt is always given to them for the amount taken, which receipt is payable on presentation to the proper officers. They also exact payment in specie for such produce as they sell the troops, putting on a most exorbitant value at the same time. In no other country would such things be permitted; and it is manifest to all here that measures like these, if persisted in, must vitally strengthen the rebellion.

You will have heard ere this of the repulse, may be defeat, of General Banks in the valley of the Shenandoah. This reverse will certainly be magnified into undue proportions by Southern agents and their sympathisers in Europe, but the facts are simply these:—the major portion of the army under Banks has been lately withdrawn to reinforce the command of McDowell covering Washington, the latter having been greatly depleted to increase the army of the Potomac, and Banks' small force has necessarily been compelled to retire in face of largely superior numbers. It has been no secret in this army that such a movement on the part of the enemy was to be expected; for deserters, 'contrabands,' and prisoners have informed us that large reinforcements have been despatched from Richmond to aid 'Stonewall' Jackson. Why then do we not attack the enemy in front of us? It is obvious that we greatly outnumber our antagonists, or they would long ere this have made demonstrations upon our position. 'What are we waiting for?' men ask each other, and nobody volunteers to give an explanation.

CHAPTER XV.

BATTLE OF HANOVER COURT HOUSE.

I HAVE at length found out the meaning of yesterday's cannonading, and it appears that we actually attacked the enemy at Hanover Court House, with malice prepense, and won a victory. Since General McClellan took command of the army of the Potomac—now ten months ago—this is the first time he has been guilty of the indiscretion of assuming the offensive; always excepting the fiercely contested battle of Williamsburg—but for that he was in no sense responsible, 'Fighting Joe Hooker,' as the troops delight to call him, having attacked the retreating Confederates 'on his own hook,' and, with the eventual assistance of Kearny, whipping them handsomely without McClellan's being aware that anything like fighting was in progress.

Orders were issued the night before last for Morell's division to hold itself in readiness to leave early next morning for parts unknown, the men to be in light marching order and carrying no other *impedimenta* than their canteens, india-rubber cloths, two days' rations, arms, and sixty rounds of ammunition. *Réveillée* beat at 3 A.M., the rain pouring down in torrents and utterly preventing the cooking of breakfasts; but so delighted were the troops at the chance of a brush with the enemy, that the division set off on its travels with light hearts at seven.

There was much curiosity amongst the men as to where they were bound, until it became apparent that Hanover Court House was the point of destination, news having been brought to head-quarters that the enemy had lately been concentrating troops in that vicinity, thus threatening our right flank. After marching twelve miles the enemy was reached, and the action immediately commenced. The Confederate force proved to be two brigades, composed of six North Carolina regiments, under command of a former member of Congress from that State, Lawrence O'Brian Branch, whom the exigencies of war had transformed from a civilian into a brigadier-general. Porter's force largely outnumbered his opponent's, and yet he came very near losing the day by his shameful want of common foresight. The object of his expedition was to get in between Branch and Richmond, for the purpose of destroying a portion of the Virginia Central Railroad, thus preventing reinforcements reaching his antagonist, and then to capture or destroy the force opposed to him. The destruction of the railroad was rapidly effected by the Twenty-second Massachusetts regiment; and the first part of the battle resulted in the precipitate but orderly retreat of the Confederates in a northerly direction, leaving their wounded and dead on the field. But a good joke comes in here. Branch and his troops were fresh arrivals from North Carolina, and they knew about as much of the country around Richmond as Porter himself. Taking a road which seemingly led northwards and westerly, they shortly after described a semicircle and came right upon Porter's rear, capturing his hospitals, wounded, and many of his surgeons, and producing the utmost consternation in the Union ranks. The battle recommenced with greater intensity than ever, but this time Branch was fighting with his back to Richmond and his line of retreat well open. Nevertheless, the result was the same as before; the Union troops were too numerous and determined, and Branch had to fall back at eventide, leaving many of his killed and wounded and five hundred prisoners in the hands of his antagonist.

Porter's men, who have returned to camp, are savage that the enemy has thus escaped them. They say that if Kearny or Hooker had commanded, not a rebel soldier would have got back to Richmond to tell the story. But FitzJohn Porter is the bosom friend and constant companion of McClellan, and the capture of his hospitals and wounded will therefore be hushed up, and the action at Hanover Court House heralded throughout the country as a complete success.

CHAPTER XVI.

THE BATTLE OF FAIR OAKS.*

May 31

I WRITE under great excitement around me; but a newspaper correspondent, like a general, must always 'possess his soul in peace,' and never permit any considerations for his own personal safety and ease to interfere with his photographing of events.

I must begin with the weather, for that is likely to prove an important item at the present time. It has rained incessantly during several days past, and the trumpery ditch with the long name Chickahominy ('Chicken and Hominy' the soldiers call it for short) has magnified itself into a huge river, covering the entire bed of the valley, and varying in width from a quarter of a mile to a mile. The natives hereabouts say that it takes two days to rise and three to fall; but it will be surprising indeed if the immense volume of waters in front of us can subside under a week.

Shortly after noon to-day, we were startled by a distant sound of rapid musketry and artillery firing in the direction of Bottom's Bridge. All who could leave camp immediately ran to the brow of the chain of hills between ourselves and the river; the noise increased rapidly, seeming to advance towards us, as though one army or the other were being driven, and occasionally we could hear cheering. Officers

---

* Sometimes called 'Seven Pines.'

who have seen service expressed surprise at the comparative absence of artillery, the firing being almost entirely confined to musketry; but this was in such volume and so continuous, that everybody is anxious to obtain intelligence from the scene of action. Orders have just come from head-quarters for us to be under arms to-morrow morning before daylight; and we are also informed that Heintzelman and Keyes have attacked the enemy and repulsed him at every point. The troops are in a furor of excitement, and bets are high that we shall be in Richmond by Wednesday.

June 1 (10 p.m.).

Yesterday's fighting was renewed at an early hour this morning. The whole of Franklin's corps has been vainly endeavouring all day to cross the river, the enemy having apparently disappeared from our front; but such is the height of the waters that fording is impossible, and bridge-building equally so. It was a noble and yet a pitiable sight to see the splendid regiments and brigades of this *corps d'armée* marching in serried columns to the edge of the river, and vainly endeavouring to reach the other side; far as the eye could reach the numerous bodies of men studded the banks, while countless horsemen hurried to and fro, seeking evidently for some unknown means of crossing.

Late in the afternoon we heard rumours which seriously controvert the news of yesterday's success. Faces look downcast to-night, for if the intelligence be correct, the *corps d'armée* under General Keyes has been driven back in disorder several miles, and one of his divisions absolutely annihilated. The fighting to-day has been more favourable to our arms, at least so it is reported;

but nobody seems inclined to credit the assurance without confirmation. The artillery firing has been much greater this day than yesterday, and evidently farther removed from us; but we must await news from head-quarters before making up our minds as to who are the victors.

June 2.

The truth is leaking out at last. The day before yesterday the enemy, taking advantage of the unprecedented rise in the Chickahominy, surprised the division under General Casey, driving it from its works and capturing its camps and artillery. From the reports of my different informants I gather that the Confederates have achieved a perfect surprise, suddenly rushing into our works at the point of the bayonet, capturing all the guns and turning them upon our troops. The second division of the *corps*, under Couch, managed to hold its works until reinforcements arrived at double-quick from Hooker and Kearny; but so overwhelming were the numbers and determination of the enemy that, had it not been for the unexpected appearance of Sumner's divisions, the entire of the Union army south of the Chickahominy might have been driven pell-mell into White Oak Swamp. By dint of almost superhuman exertions, 'Old Bull Sumner,' as he is called in the army, managed to get his divisions somehow across the swollen river, and arrived just in time to save us from defeat, and to turn a terrible repulse into almost a victory. Yesterday morning the engagement was renewed by mutual consent of both parties, and we have really achieved a triumph, the enemy being driven in disorder at all points, and the Union lines considerably advanced towards Richmond.

Many who have hitherto defended General McClellan

against all critics, assuming that his dilatoriness and adverseness to attack were the result of deep-laid strategy, now find their faith in him seriously shaken. The disaster to Casey's division on Saturday was solely due to McClellan's fearful want of foresight; for not merely were the men composing that command the rawest and least disciplined in the army, but the division was thrown forward so egregiously in advance of all supports, that a mere tyro might have known it was in danger of being cut off by the enemy. Worse even than this was the isolating one half of his army from the remainder by keeping Porter's, Franklin's, and Sumner's corps on the northern bank of the Chickahominy, and those of Keyes and Heintzelman across the stream. With a rise in the river—always to be looked for at this season of the year—the enemy can throw the whole of his force upon one half or the other of our army; for he holds the upper waters of the stream, with numerous fords and bridges, whilst we have not a picket beyond the Virginia Central Railroad, nor any means by which to obtain a knowledge of his intentions. Doubtless it will be our turn to receive his visit the next; and yet we have no works whatever by which to defend ourselves against a movement on our right flank.*

* Nothing will better show McClellan's entire ignorance of the movements of his command than his despatches to the Secretary of War upon this engagement. Writing from New Bridge on June 5, he says:—'My telegraphic despatch of June 1, in regard to the Battle of Fair Oaks, was incorrectly published in the papers. I send with this a correct copy, which I request may be published at once. I am the more anxious about this, since my despatch, as published, would seem to ignore the services of Gen. Sumner, which were too valuable and brilliant to be overlooked, both in the difficult passage of the stream and the subsequent combat.' Now the fact is, the papers published the despatch in question as his chief-of-staff gave it to them; and it was only when, *days afterwards*, McClellan got to be acquainted with the details of the action, that he saw the omission he had

CHAPTER XVII.

IN SIGHT OF RICHMOND.

MECHANICSVILLE (4½ miles from Richmond):
June 6.

THE First New Jersey brigade changed its quarters yesterday from New Bridge to this place, a charming little village on the banks of the now famous Chickahominy. Before General Kearny assumed command of Hamilton's division at the siege of Yorktown, the Jersey brigade held the position of honour in the army of the Potomac, being the first brigade in the first division of the first *corps d'armée*. Kearny's promotion, however, and the assignment of General Franklin to the newly-created sixth corps, have changed it from the first to the last, and it is now the last brigade in the last division of the last *corps d'armée*. Notwithstanding this alteration, due to the fact of seniority of other officers, it is still at the post of honour, being on the extreme right of the line, and guarding the most vulnerable point also.

made, and hastened to rectify it. The case is precisely similar to that of Kearny at Williamsburg; but McClellan's conduct in reference to the battle of Fair Oaks is even worse, for he imputes blame to Casey's division when the fault of its repulse was simply his own. His invariable absence from the field of battle, his partiality for certain officers, and unjust ignoring of others, very naturally upset the popularity manufactured so studiously for him by certain politicians and newspapers. At the present day he has few supporters in the army other than the Irish, and they are obviously attracted by the euphony of his Celtic name.

We reached Mechanicsville yesterday afternoon, and immediately proceeded to clean and occupy a deserted camping ground of the enemy in the woods, beside the road leading to the river. I forthwith started to prospect the adjoining country, and, still more, to catch a glimpse of that city which is the goal of all our labours. The 'pike' (turnpike) runs through this apology for a village by a gentle descent to the river, and there crosses it by a small bridge, distant from Mechanicsville a good half-mile, if not three-quarters; the other side, the ground rises rapidly, the hills south of the stream being much bolder and loftier than on the north, and less wooded. The spires of the Richmond churches are plainly visible from the village with the naked eye, and the sound of bells and the railroad whistle may easily be heard. Close to the bridge there is a signpost bearing the information, 'To Richmond, four and a quarter miles.'

The bridge is a wooden structure. Almost everything in this Southern country seems to be merely wooden and temporary, as though the people did not believe it could last, or are waiting for some great change. The '*Old Dominion*' is no exception to the rule. You occasionally come across some substantial looking venerable brick structure, with an unmistakable English appearance about it, but with these very scarce exceptions everything else is temporary, wooden, and fragile. The former buildings mark the period of Virginia's prosperity—the era of her Washingtons, Jeffersons, and Madisons; the latter, the time of her decadence—the period of her Hunters, Masons, Wises, 'nigger breeding,' and Fugitive Slave Law. But to return to the bridge over the Chickahominy. Two rows of strong piles are driven into the bed of the stream; thick beams run from these to either shore, and others again are placed from pile to pile, forming together a bridge some forty feet long by about fifteen wide. That portion of the structure between our bank and the first row of piles has been broken away, but a single three-inch-thick plank rests loosely in its place, as though inviting a visit from our side. I feel much inclined to try a walk across, merely for the say-so of the thing; but I don't want to go to Richmond without the rest of my friends.

What may be General McClellan's object in holding this place, is more than ever a mystery to all here. Early this morning I was informed that the upper slope of the hills, the other side of the river, was crowded with the enemy's working parties; I immediately stepped out from the woods into the open, and found the rebels busily engaged in throwing up redoubts and breastworks on either side the road. We have a section of artillery pointing towards the bridge, and I asked the officer in command whether these working parties in such beautiful shelling range were to be let alone. He replied that no orders had been given to interfere with their operations, but for his own part he considered it a crying shame to let such a chance pass without a little practising for his men. I walked over to the head-quarters of General Taylor, commanding the brigade, and learned from him, much to my surprise and his own ill-concealed disgust, that his orders were precise ' not to interfere in any way with the enemy's operations.' Doubtless the order is dictated by sound, deep strategy; but it seemed to me and many others, that if we held the hills in front of us, we should have an admirable position for flanking the enemy fronting Heintzelman and Keyes, threatening Richmond closely at the same time. While the rebels are thus working, we are lying idle in camp; and when their redoubts are completed and siege guns mounted, we shall have to evacuate Mechanicsville at full speed.

The other division of this corps crossed the Chickahominy on Thursday, and when we left New Bridge it was safely encamped on the right bank of the river. General Sumner had extended his front towards us, so as to cover the crossing, and it may be in McClellan's plans to advance his line still further in this direction, so as to cover the approaches to Richmond at this place. It becomes a more difficult matter every day to learn when the general advance will be made, and every successive move still further mystifies us. There are a thousand and one rumours about the camps, and a man need be inspired to detect the truth in so vast a mass of error. Certain facts however leak out, which, if known to most, are not allowed to appear in the Northern journals; as, for instance, the arrival of large reinforcements by way of York River, and the placing of heavy siege guns in position on the centre of our lines. These are the 100lb. rifled guns which proved themselves so valuable at Yorktown. They are brought by water to West Point, and thence transported by rail to the front of the army.

I should judge from this fact that McClellan intends a similar advance upon Richmond to that made upon Corinth by Halleck; else why this seeming delay, which may benefit the enemy almost, if not quite, as much as himself? Beauregard's western army being now broken up, it is more than probable that portions of it at least will be brought here to reinforce Davis and Johnston. Halleck telegraphs that none had left the neighbourhood of Corinth up to a certain day, but I am satisfied the result will prove the contrary. During the whole of last night and to-day the arrival of trains at Richmond has been unceasing, and I feel confident the rebel leaders are massing troops at this point who formerly were a portion of Beauregard's command. These reinforcements have not come by the direct route, General Mitchell having cut off 200 miles of the Memphis and Charleston railroad; but it was comparatively easy for them to reach Richmond by the Mobile and Ohio line, although with great loss of time. They would descend to Southern Alabama, and then take the lines running towards Virginia; but, as will be seen by reference to a map, the distance is so great that no very large proportion of Beauregard's army could arrive here in time for the impending battle.

We hear, but cannot verify the information, that Heintzelman has crossed the James River, and that Petersburg is in process of evacuation: this may account for a late order of the Secretary of War extending McClellan's command to Weldon, in North Carolina, and including Fortress Monroe. Those in the way of obtaining more information than others, assert that this army has increased its numbers in consequence by 25,000 men during the past week; but the lines are so extensive, and prominent officers so ambiguous or reticent, that it is an impossibility to verify the statement. That very large reinforcements are daily arriving, I know however to be correct.

The enemy opened upon us at New Bridge the day before yesterday, and gave us a very pretty specimen of artillery practice during some three hours. The banks of the Chickahominy seem almost to have been made for such practice, either side of the river rising rapidly and affording sufficient 'open' for field and other batteries. The distance from height to height varies from 1,200 yards to 3,000 yards; and should the fire become too hot, the gunners may retreat into the woods at their rear, and find perfect security in the hollow. I watched the artillery duel of Thursday with much interest, particularly as the practice of the enemy was much better than I had hitherto seen. They fired rapidly, and changed the position of their field pieces so frequently as to lead many to suppose their strength was double what it really was. No infantry showed themselves, and it required but a small amount of penetration to see that their object was merely to learn the position of our batteries, and perhaps our strength in artillery. Here, however, they were deceived; for the reply on our side was made by two batteries only, our range proving greatly superior to theirs. We have thirty field batteries of six guns each at this point, two-thirds of them being rifled ten, twenty, and thirty pounders. Only one man on our side was killed, his death occurring from the bursting of a shell; the Prince de Joinville, the Count of Paris, General McClellan, and other notabilities, being near the battery at the time.

The four regiments composing this brigade have received orders to be under arms to-morrow morning (Sunday) at 3 A.M. Generals FitzJohn Porter and Franklin came over to Mechanicsville this afternoon, and examined the enemy's position during half an hour. Putting this fact with our anticipated early rising on the morrow, and taking into consideration the apparently purposeless firing of the enemy on Thursday, and their choice of Sunday for attacks, I feel somewhat anxious about the morning. It is now eleven o'clock at night; but notwithstanding the late hour, the discharges of artillery are frequent on our left, and I occasionally hear distant musketry. Should my anticipations prove correct of a contest to-morrow, the point of attack will not be far removed from this place. McClellan's head-quarters are still at New Bridge, four miles east of

Mechanicsville; and when we left there yesterday he had 30,000 men under his immediate eye, and thirty batteries of field artillery. Our brigade numbers about 3,200 effectives, and we have here three batteries of rifled guns. Stoneman, with about an equal force, a portion being cavalry, is some two miles north of us, and the telegraphic wire puts us in instantaneous communication with McClellan. Our best safeguard is the swollen, deep Chickahominy in front of us, otherwise our little force could not hold this position for any length of time.

A flag of truce came over from the enemy yesterday, the object being to inquire after the health of the wounded General Pettigrew, captured last Sunday in the battle of Fair Oaks. This general is a South Carolinian, and the son of a former governor of that State, who bears the reputation of being opposed to Secession. The Pettigrews are among the wealthiest planters in Cottondom, and the family played an important part in the revolutionary war. The Pettigrew of that period made himself remarkable by enunciating the opinion in the first Congress, that *there ought to be no New Yorkers or South Carolinians, but only 'Americans.'* Strangely has his descendant fallen away from the faith when he is thus found battling in defence of the doctrine of States' rights, and seeking to break up a nation which his grandsire endeavoured to consolidate. The bearers of the flag of truce brought us news that General Joseph Johnston was wounded in the battle of Sunday last, and that General Robert Lee has been appointed commander-in-chief of the rebel 'Army of Virginia.' As Johnston was their principal commander, the Confederates are scarcely likely to claim the battle as a victory. A gentleman, lately arrived from the field of action, informed me that the loss of life during the two days was enormous; three days after the fight, he saw hundreds of bodies lying in the woods, and beneath the abattis—the Confederate uniform more than doubling that of their opponents. Sixteen hundred had already been interred by the Union troops, and yet it seemed to him as though none had been buried, so much remained to be done. My informant is of the opinion that our own losses were much larger than at first supposed—namely, 2,500 killed, wounded, and missing; he thinks 4,000 would be much nearer the mark.*

The weather in Virginia at this season is most disagreeable, and dangerous to the health of the troops. Three or four broiling hot days, with the thermometer nearly 90 degrees, are succeeded by cold, wet, easterly winds, which produce intermittent and congestive complaints; add to this the malaria from the swamps of the Chickahominy, and you will readily understand that campaigning is not quite so *couleur de rose* as romancers love to paint it. I have hitherto managed to keep your correspondent in a moderate degree of health, but it is only by a liberal use of prophylactics. There is a story told of a cat, which had been fed so long by a soldier on pipeclay and water that she would not touch milk. I have almost persuaded myself that I like quinine, in doses amounting to ten grains per diem. Verily, campaigning hath its bitters!

June 9.

Contrary to general expectation, the enemy permitted us to pass Sunday in peace. They, however, worked hard

---

* It is now admitted by the Confederates that McClellan might have marched into Richmond after the battle of Fair Oaks with the greatest ease. They were utterly astonished at his unaccountable delay in following up his victory.

all day, if we may judge by that portion of their army encamped in front of us; and, much to the surprise of our men and officers, they were permitted to continue their fortifications without let or hindrance on our part. Nobody here, not even the general commanding the brigade, can give the reason for our permitting these works to continue; instructions from head-quarters confine us to holding this bank of the river, forbidding our firing at passing bodies of their troops, their pickets, or fortifications. This morning they are throwing up another work on the opposite side of the road, and when this is complete they will have a cross-fire at the bridge from half a mile distance, which will keep back any force of infantry.

The main body of the enemy here is hidden behind a belt of trees; but we can see their white tents beyond when the sun passes the meridian. They have largely increased their force within the past twenty-four hours, two encampments showing up between the hills further to our right. They seem, indeed, to design turning our flank two or three miles higher up the river, or, may be, they are preparing to communicate with the retreating army of 'Stonewall' Jackson, falling back before Fremont and Banks. Stoneman's two regiments of cavalry and his light artillery are watching them continually, and our own brigade now pickets up the river for two miles beyond where the Virginia Central Railroad crosses the Chickahominy. I think our picketing is on far too profuse a scale, both as regards distance and numbers, twelve companies out of a single brigade doing duty along four miles of front. It was such a fault as this, isolating squads of men from support, which led to General Casey's misfortune at the battle of Saturday week.

Our pickets and those of the enemy are in close proximity to each other at the bridge, scarcely three hundred yards intervening between them. There seems to be a mutual desire to let each other alone for the present, although batteries are gaping on every height, and our men at least are 'spoiling for a fight.' There are courtesies and amenities even in warfare, and until the moment when Federals and Confederates are ordered to cut each other's throats, we treat each other with 'distinguished consideration,' as diplomatists have it. The bridge at Mechanicsville is neutral ground, no 'villanous saltpetre' disturbing the long-continued harmony. Yesterday, a private of the Third New Jersey Regiment ran along the bridge towards the enemy, waving in his hand a New York paper of the 6th inst.; he was met half-way by a Confederate major, who gave him in exchange a copy of the *Richmond Dispatch* of the 7th, which has since been forwarded to General M'Clellan. The New York paper contained General Halleck's despatch relating to the evacuation of Corinth and his capture of 10,000 prisoners and 15,000 stand of arms. 'What,' said the Major, 'Corinth evacuated! that is indeed news!' Numerous little episodes like the above frequently transpire here, and have a tendency to make war appear much less horrible than the reality. A week ago some of our pickets at New Bridge were boiling coffee in the woods on the banks of the river, when a Confederate soldier creeped down towards them and called out, 'What are you doing there, boys?' 'Hallo! we're making a cup of coffee,' was the reply. 'Is it real coffee, now?' came back to them from the opposite bank. 'Yes,' the picket answered. 'If I leave my gun here and swim across, will you give me some, and let me return again?' said the rebel soldier. 'All right,' was the answer, and the murky gray uniform of a Confederate shortly joined the picket, and put itself outside a pint of the infusion. A hearty meal of biscuit and cold pork caused the rebel to reflect upon the copiousness of 'Union' rations as compared with his own, and he told his new friends, 'We don't get enough to eat on the other side. I think I sha'n't go back again.' Thereupon the officer of the guard was called, and the deserter was subsequently marched to head-quarters. The bottom of the valley in the neighbourhood of New Bridge is a conglomeration of thickly-wooded islets, swamps, and water-courses. Occasionally during the day and evening were heard the sounds of clarionet from the middle of this morass, the amateur awakening the echoes with 'Dixie,' the 'Marseillaise,' and other airs fashionable amongst 'Secesh.' Two or three rifle-shots from our pickets on the river had little effect upon the player beyond making him change his tunes; for he would reply with 'Yankee-Doodle,' 'Hail Columbia,' or the 'Star-spangled Banner,' receiving a volley from the other side in answer. Who this strange individual is, nobody knows. I have set her down (it must be *her*) as some Naiad or Dryad fresh from Arcadia, or Minnehaha calling her lost Hiawatha.

We had unexpected visitors at our camp yesterday—five ladies, who did us the honour of passing several hours in our company, attending Divine service with us in the evening. Four of them were black as the proverbial ace of spades, with high cheek-bones, thick features, shiny skins, and wonderfully bright eyes full of humour and life; they were dressed in cast-off clothes of their owners, but wore no bonnets, and the thick shoes on their enormous feet told us they were field hands. The fifth was 'yellow,' though if I were called upon to define her hue I should define her as a bad-complexioned white-skin with an incurable affection of the liver; I judged her to be an 'amalgamation' between a mulatto woman and white man, the 'tar-brush' showing itself mainly in the features. She evidently possessed full authority over the others, they conceding her right to command them without opposition or murmur, and she informed us that her owner, a widow, had run off when our forces approached, leaving her mistress of the situation. These much-oppressed slaves certainly evince a remarkable degree of fidelity towards their owners, in spite of the ill-treatment continually vented upon them. We were all astonished to hear that female 'chattels,' grown-up women, are frequently ordered to strip themselves to the skin, and then receive blows from whips or cowhides according to the temper of their owners. The coloured girl above told us, 'We (meaning those of her light complexion) give more trouble than the rest, for we are very much like the white folk, and don't like being put upon. My mistress said the other day, before you came, she was cursed with a lot of smart niggers, and I guess she is too.' In answer to our inquiries, she told us that some of our troops had carried off the fowls on the plantation, and stolen some of the vegetables; 'but,' she added, 'I don't complain much, for I dare say the poor fellows are tired of hard biscuit, and we should do the same.' She was very pleased to hear that a guard would be placed over the premises in future, and that all produce should be paid for on removal from the plantation.

We obtained a full insight into the much-vaunted slave system of Virginia from these girls. Their chief complaint was that their relatives were taken from them and sold South; two of them were minus their husbands from this cause. No regard whatever seems to be paid to their religious interests, none of them having attended Divine worship since they were little children. When we told them there would be service in the regiment after parade, and that they were welcome to be present, they evinced much curiosity, and their attention and glances at each other during the performance proved how novel it was to them. We learned from them that our rapid advance in this direction had prevented their owners carrying them off, and they promised us visits from many others of their class as soon as our presence became known through the country. So it is wherever the Northern armies march, and the slave-owners know it full well, for they drive off their field hands and house servants, fearing the demoralising influence of the abolitionist Yankees. We are hailed as deliverers, and yet the negroes seem to regard freedom as nothing more than the right to go where they choose, and to keep all the money they can make by their labour. I have not yet met a single one with the first idea of political advantage accruing to him from this much-desired liberty. An elderly coloured man said to me to-day, with no small amount of humour and sarcasm, ' These niggers will begin to think before long they are human.'

10 P.M.

We hear good news to-night, and from authority, too, which we assuredly ought not to doubt. General M'Dowell has received orders to join us here without further delay, and there is therefore some probability at last of his approach being more than a rumour. Some of my late letters may have led you to believe that he had already left Fredericksburg with this object ; such was the belief of all here, and much astonishment has been shown at his strange delay.

June 10.

We sent a flag of truce across the river to-day for the purpose of giving up four ladies captured by General Stoneman's advance corps some fortnight ago. The ladies in question were Mrs. Lee, wife of General Robert Lee, her two daughters, and a visitor at their house when they were taken. Colonel Torbert* of the 1st New Jersey Regiment, being the officer of the day, was deputed to accompany them outside our lines; in other words, across the Meadow bridge over the Chickahominy, two miles from this village. The ladies were very affable and pleasant, but no reference whatever was made on either side to any political matters. The party was stopped on the Confederate side of the river, and we learned that a Virginia regiment was guarding the position under the orders of General Heth. One of the officers expressed to Colonel Torbert his satisfaction at seeing the old uniform again. There are doubtless many others who feel like him, and only require the opportunity to show their true sentiments.

We learn that the celebrated cavalry officer Ashby was killed in the late battle between Jackson and Fremont, and that 'an English adventurer, whom Lincoln had made a colonel of cavalry,' was captured in the same engagement. The *Richmond Enquirer* gives his name as Sir Percy Worden, but means Wyndham: this gentleman served under Garibaldi in Italy, and now commands the 1st New Jersey Cavalry in the Union army.

June 11.

This day week is the anniversary of the battle of Waterloo, and it would not be surprising if McClellan

---

* Now *Major-General* Torbert, chief of Sheridan's cavalry.

should select it as the day on which his advance will be made. The Confederate army is in the position of our own covering Brussels, and the country hereabouts is not dissimilar to that around the village of Waterloo, except that it is more hilly. 'Stonewall' Jackson may answer for Blucher—he has shown himself as brave and dashing as the Prussian—and M'Dowell may turn out another Grouchy, if the report of his slowness be correct. There is, as yet, no appearance of any part of his army moving, and reinforcements are continually arriving by way of York River. M'Dowell has not shown up, and we are never permitted to know anything of his whereabouts. It has poured down rain in torrents during the last thirty-six hours, and not merely is the Chickahominy higher than ever, and the swamps lakes, but the hills on which we are encamped have become morasses where the foot sinks in to the ancle. Surely the skies are in league with the enemy!

11 P.M.

The reason of our strange delay of the past week is now explained. General M'Clellan has been seriously ill, and, I am informed, so seriously as to cause fears for his safety. Not the slightest suspicion of this fact has leaked out in the army; and no better proof can be required of the secrecy with which military operations here are conducted than that such a fact has been kept secret in the camp during upwards of a week. I hear that the General was over the river to-day, but have no means of establishing the truth of the report; a friend of mine just returned from head-quarters states to me he was so informed there.

June 12.

We were greatly surprised by a visit from General McClellan this afternoon; he was accompanied by Generals

Franklin and Porter, and a numerous suite; amongst whom were the Prince de Joinville, and Colonels Neville and Fletcher, of our Household Brigade. The young General-in-Chief certainly looked very little like a sick man, although but a few days ago he was in such a state as to alarm his friends. Many here will not believe he has been sick at all, but simply that he has been playing the 'old soldier' for strategic reasons. He was dressed in as *négligé* a costume as one might desire this hot weather: a loose blue woollen blouse, jack-boots and straw hat; nothing in fact would lead one to suppose he had any connection with the army. The party on arriving here ascended the hill overlooking the enemy's position, between our camps and the river, and passed half-an-hour in reconnoitring the lately-thrown-up breastworks and redoubts of the rebels. The horses were left out of sight, and McClellan, Franklin and Porter, leaving their suite in the rear, walked some distance along the heights, and finally climbed to the roof of a high barn, whence the valley of the Chickahominy may be traced for miles. A flag of truce from the enemy was the principal cause of this visit. An officer of the 2nd Jersey regiment, on duty with his company at what is known as the Meadow-bridge, received the flag this morning; the letter was immediately despatched to head-quarters, and must have contained matter of importance to bring the General so far along the lines to reply to it. The Confederate officer bearing the flag of truce proved to be a scion of the Virginia house of Mason, and a nephew of the Confederate plenipotentiary now in England; a short conversation with our own officer gave us important information—that is, if the former's statements be well founded. He declared laughingly that Richmond was in no more danger of capture than

Washington, and that the fight would not come off in this vicinity at all, but in Fairfax county; in other words, near the celebrated lines of Manassas. This may be the usual Southern bombast; but I, for one, shall not be surprised if there be something of the kind attempted after all. An extract from a Mississippi paper, republished in the *Richmond Enquirer*, asserted the same thing within the past week. M'Clellan's army now stretches from the James River to the Chickahominy, his right flank resting on the Virginia Central Railroad. Drawing a line from the point where this road crosses the Chickahominy, to White House on the Pamunkey, we have, as nearly as necessary, the line of demarcation between the enemy's forces and our own—the country south being occupied by us, while all north and west is open to the Confederates. What is to prevent the latter leaving Richmond and marching either to meet Jackson or to the relief of Fredericksburg?

M'Dowell has been heard from, and perhaps the movements of his army may induce the Confederates to make such an attempt. One of the three divisions composing his corps has already landed at White House (the point where the Richmond and West Point Railroad crosses the Pamunkey River); the second is said to be on its way by the same route, the Chesapeake and York Rivers; whilst the third is marching southward from Fredericksburg, and will, I learn, join us in this direction. Central Virginia is thus comparatively free, the force until lately opposed to M'Dowell having probably been marched back upon the capital. The armies under Fremont, Banks, Sigel, and Shields, numbering some 60,000 men, are following up Jackson through the valley of the Shenandoah. The enemy may have learnt of M'Dowell's evacuation of Fredericksburg, and the prospect of his arrival here, and they are not unlikely to effect a diversion towards the Rappahannock, especially as by so doing they may assist Jackson, and stop the advance of M'Dowell's third division. Forewarned is forearmed. Maybe McClellan has prepared for this contingency.

June 13.

We changed our camping ground at sunrise this morning, moving up the Chickahominy a distance of about a quarter of a mile. Our present location is in a wood, where the dead leaves lie half a foot in depth, and the insects are more numerous and ugly than ever.

Towards noon, our brigade received orders to hold itself in readiness to march at a moment's notice, and we soon after learned that we were to join our division and cross the Chickahominy at what is known as Sumner's bridge, four miles below Newbridge. About four o'clock, however, we were informed that the enemy were in force at Old Church, seven or eight miles in our rear, and word was sent for the troops to be prepared to advance in light marching order, leaving waggons and baggage under as small a guard as possible. Thus stand matters at present, and we have the prospect of a night march and tough work in the morning. Old Church lies between Hanover Court House and Cold Harbour, and the enemy thus threatens our dépôt at White House on the Pamunkey River, and the railroad by which supplies are forwarded for all our army on the Chickahominy. I trust that I may be mistaken, but there certainly appears to have been an awful ' mull ' somewhere.

June 14.

After closing my record of last evening, we received orders countermanding those previously given. We have quietly remained inside our lines all day, and the enemy have been remarkably affable towards us.

The information received here relative to the affairs of yesterday has a very black appearance. The following are the facts so far as known. A Confederate force, composed of six regiments of infantry and two of cavalry, has turned our right flank, and got completely in our rear, between the Chickahominy and Pamunkey, burnt two schooners laden with stores on the latter river, and penetrated as far as Tunstall's station on the Richmond and West Point Railroad, where the attempt was then made to destroy the bridges. A heavily-laden train, carrying stores to the main portion of the army, was fired into at this point, and would infallibly have been captured if, according to custom, it had stopped to water at Tunstall's. A waggon train coming by the 'pike road from White House was almost entirely destroyed; fifty of these huge vehicles being burnt or otherwise damaged, the teamsters and guards killed, and the horses driven off. Such are the details of this daring and well-executed feat of the rebels in the very rear of our army.

Further intelligence may modify these particulars, but there can be no washing out the blackness of the affair so far as concerns the main facts. The enemy reached the Pamunkey River in the vicinity of White House, and attacked the most vulnerable portion of the solitary railroad by which we receive the supplies of our army; in other words, they turn our flank and get nearly twenty miles back in our rear without anybody to check them and obviously without anybody being aware of their presence. Officers of high rank complain grievously of this want of foresight on the part of their superiors, and are fiercely, and most justly so, too, severe on the management of a campaign which permits such a person as Mrs. Lee, the wife of the principal rebel general, to pass through our lines, and, of course, to carry information to the enemy. It is almost self-evident that the Confederate raid has been planned upon this lady's information, obtained, be it remembered, while she remained a prisoner at White House. Mrs. Lee had every attention shown her, being escorted by cavalry in triumph to the rebel lines. Certain United States' officers are wonderfully kid-gloved with these Southern aristocrats; but from what I have seen and heard to-day I am satisfied the army does not appreciate such politeness.

Two deserters swam the Chickahominy this afternoon, and gave themselves up to our pickets. I was present at their examination, and found they belonged to the Louisiana brigade, but were both natives of New York State. They informed us there are numbers of Northern men who have been forced into the Southern ranks, and are now seeking to get to the front so as to effect their escape. Like the prisoners with whom I have conversed, they represent the force in front of Richmond to be constantly receiving large additions, and they report also a deficiency in rations.

Midnight.

Word has just come in that the enemy have crossed the Chickahominy, and are in force on our right flank. There is therefore every prospect of an engagement at this point before daylight. General McClellan moved his quarters across the river the day before yesterday, *away from the threatened point*, and we have now only three divisions and the brigade of regulars north of the Chickahominy, a force of about 35,000 men. The place is evidently becoming too hot to hold us much longer, thanks to our senseless delay and the time we have given the enemy to hurry up overwhelming reinforcements. It almost looks as though we were playing his game knowingly.

June 16.

Our expectations of an attack yesterday were doomed to disappointment, and we now learn that one of our own signal officers was the cause of the 'scare.' It appears that the individual in question telegraphed from this end of our lines to General McClellan, without communicating with anybody here, and upon his information we were warned from head-quarters to hold ourselves in readiness for an attack. The day passed off, however, without the enemy showing themselves, and we enjoyed one of the quietest Sundays of the campaign.

Further intelligence relative to the late Confederate raid in our rear places the affair in a still more brilliant light for the enemy, and damaging one for ourselves. Our pickets captured a newsboy this morning, carrying Richmond papers to the rebel troops: he had unintentionally strayed within our lines, bringing under his arm a bundle of the *Richmond Dispatch*, and you may be sure our soldiers seized upon the booty with avidity. The papers contained a two-and-a-half column report of the dashing feat performed by the enemy in our rear, and written, too, with little of the usual Southern bombast and exaggerations; the affair, in truth, requires no colouring whatever, being sufficiently romantic in itself to be spared the attention of sensation writers. Apart from the ingenious manner in which the story is related, I learn from officers and others who have been over the road in the wake of the enemy that all the truth is not told in the Richmond paper; true, the

Dispatch sets down the value of the property destroyed at three millions of dollars, but if our losses do not reach this sum, it is sufficient to know that upwards of one million are admitted as the minimum. Two hundred four-horse waggons were destroyed, many prisoners taken, and scores of valuable horses driven off; yet these losses, considerable as they appear, are the lightest we have sustained by the enemy's inroad.

The evident object of the Confederate generals was to learn, by reconnoitring, the extent of our force between the Pamunkey and Chickahominy rivers, and for this purpose a force was put under General Stuart, consisting of six regiments of infantry, two of cavalry, and two field-pieces. This little army, it would appear, left Richmond by the north, and marched straight to Old Church, between Hanover Court House and Cold Harbour, reaching that point after driving in our cavalry pickets about Thursday morning. The cavalry and field-pieces pushed on henceforward alone. The former numbered in all 1,400 men, and were portions of four regiments, the colonels of two of them being sons of General Lee. They first of all made for the Pamunkey River, where they burned a couple of schooners laden with forage, and were only deterred from attacking the dépôt of all our supplies by the fear of finding a large force at White House. There was nothing of the sort, however, incredible as it may appear; and they might just as well have destroyed all our stores for anything we could have done to prevent them. From the river to the station on the West Point Railroad, called Tunstall's, their march was a scene of ruin and devastation; everybody was alarmed, regiment after regiment was sent in pursuit, but none came up with them; and they ultimately crossed the Chickahominy near Bottom's Bridge, in the very rear of the centre of the Federal army now investing Richmond.

In accordance with custom in this army, the blame of this irruption is thrown upon a subordinate—Brigadier-General Cooke. On our extreme right, fronting the enemy, the 1st New Jersey Brigade holds the left side of the Virginia Central Railroad, near the Chickahominy; Major-General Stoneman takes up the defence in our rear, and General Cooke has the remainder of the line back to the Pamunkey. Cooke, I understand, has never thrown out pickets, confining himself to patrols; but he states in defence that picketing was never required of him in his orders. General Stoneman, a most admirable officer, and worthy a far more important command than he has hitherto possessed, twice complained of Cooke's failure to throw out pickets; so that others are also to blame—not Cooke alone. This officer could have no charge of the country near Bottom's Bridge, nor at Tunstall's Station, and I understand that Sumner and Hooker and Kearny charge the entire blame upon McClellan. Be the fault where it may, the enemy has made a splendid dash through the country in our rear, and learned exactly our force between the Chickahominy and Pamunkey rivers. To make the affair stranger than ever, the rebel commander, Stuart, is the son-in-law of Cooke, and the two Lees are the sons of the lady whom we put across our lines a few days ago.

This Confederate raid might have been prevented, if our generals had reconnoitred on our right flank, instead of depending upon balloon observations for knowledge of the enemy's movements. These balloons may be very efficient in a level and open country, but they are of far less utility in the vicinity of Richmond; the land is exceedingly hilly and wooded, and it is next to impossible to see anything from an elevation of one thousand feet—the extreme height of the balloon's elevations; besides which, the weather has lately been too boisterous for aëronautic operations. I question much whether ballooning has been of any advantage to the Army of the Potomac during the war, while it has certainly made the enemy much more cautious.

June 18.

We were awakened before daylight this morning, and ordered to prepare to march for some point or other the moment we were relieved. At sunrise a brigade belonging to FitzJohn Porter's corps surrounded our camping ground, guarding carefully against being seen by the enemy on the other side of the river. Unfortunately, however, our waggons were absent after supplies, and as it was impossible for them to get back until night-time, our relief returned whence they came, leaving us a fixture at this place. The men complain bitterly of what they regard as their bad luck, but we are in hopes we shall quit Mechanicsville some time to-morrow. I hear that McCall's division of the Pennsylvania reserves (8,500 strong, with 30 guns) will in future occupy this point. The command in question belongs to M'Dowell's *corps d'armée*, and reached White House from the North a few days ago. They were at Dispatch station, on the Chickahominy, this morning, and we shall probably see them at Mechanicsville during the night.

The rebels across the river seem most desirous of letting us alone, employing all their time in throwing up redoubts and breastworks on the hills in front of us. We are not permitted to interfere with their labours, to the no small astonishment of everybody here; but we put it down to

that mysterious thing called 'strategy,' although some
define it by a bad name. Deserters come in daily, all
belonging to Louisiana regiments: they creep down to the
edge of the river, wave a handkerchief to our pickets, and
then wade or swim across. One of them told us to-day
that a general order on desertion was read at parade last
night, their troops being assured the Yankees would mal-
treat them even if they managed to cross the stream. If
we may believe these deserters, all the Louisiana regiments
are more or less disaffected, the men watching their
opportunity to reach the banks of the Chickahominy.
Perhaps the fall of New Orleans may have something to
do with this demoralisation.

We learn an important fact from these deserters—
General Lee, the new general-in-chief of the Confederates,
has lately moved his head-quarters to the left of his line,
nearly opposite the point where the Virginia Central Railroad crosses the Chickahominy. This fact, in conjunction
with the great increase of camps in that direction, induces
some of our principal engineer officers to believe that a
change is about to be made in the enemy's lines. Does the
change look as though any evacuation of Richmond were
intended? The chiefs of the Federal army express the
most supreme confidence that Richmond will be held: but
this was also General Heintzelman's conviction with regard
to Yorktown the very day before it was evacuated. Jefferson
Davis said lately he could carry on a war during twenty
years in this State, and many here believe he is preparing
for such a struggle by changing his front to the Kanawha
Canal, running from Richmond towards Lynchburg and the
Shenandoah Valley, following the course of the James
River. It may not be necessary to sacrifice his capital to
this plan of operations; and holding that canal and the

country south and west of it, he may protract the campaign through the summer and winter months, and hope to gain his ends by political complications in the interim. The next eight days will probably decide the question, for McClellan has now got every regiment he has so long demanded, and his entrenchments I hear are within a day or two of completion.

CHAPTER XVIII.

ON THE CENTRE.

South of the Chickahominy, in Front of Richmond: June 20.

We left Mechanicsville yesterday morning, marched all day through a boiling-hot sun, and reached our present camping ground towards nightfall. We are now encamped at eight or ten miles' distance from Richmond, but nevertheless considerably nearer to the rebel capital and the enemy than at any period of our march; in other words, we are on the direct road to Richmond, and we must fight hard to get any nearer. The other two brigades of our division crossed the Chickahominy on Wednesday, and FitzJohn Porter's corps and M'Call's division are now the only portion of M'Clellan's army north of the river. We hear they have received orders to join us immediately, and are only waiting until King's division of M'Dowell's corps reaches them from White House. M'Clellan will then have twelve divisions in front of Richmond, besides the reinforcements arrived from the North during the past three weeks, but I found it impossible to learn what is the gross total of this immense army. Some say 100,000 men, others 150,000, but those are silent who could speak authoritatively. We have at all events enough to win; but we shall have to fight hard, very hard, before reaching Richmond—that is, if the enemy do not evacuate.

The road from our former camping ground at Newbridge to the Chickahominy was lined with deserted camps, the former habitations of tens of thousands of men, who are now over the little stream which circumstances have rendered famous. The country between the Pamunkey and Chickahominy bears a mournful aspect of ruin and devastation; fields of down-trodden grain, parched and withered, windowless houses, felled trees, putrid horses fouling the air, horns, bones, and hides of oxen, with whizzing myriads of flies circling spirally above the offal. At one house alone did we find a tenant, a sour-faced woman with a young family of sourer-faced children, who told me her name was M'Gee, and that there were many M'Gees in the Southern army. She was a Virginian of indubitable extraction, wizened by the influence of Southern institutions. Half of her house was given up to domestic servants—shiny, greasy-visaged blacks—and an outbuilding in the yard was tenanted by the still dirtier and more miserable offspring of the field hands. The whole establishment was stamped a curse, from the blear-eyed whites to the fat, stupid negroes. The M'Gee farm is situated on the road leading from Gaines's Mills to the Chickahominy, and on the summit of the hills looking down upon the valley through which winds the river; the road dips rapidly here until it reaches the extensive morass known as the Powhitan Swamp. A few scorchingly hot days have dried up the deep mud in the valley, and we were able to walk dry-shod upon ground which a week ago was impassable; but a mile or more of corduroyed road proved to us what difficulties were encountered by the army in its pursuit of the enemy. The road in question was admirably well constructed by the New York Volunteer Engineers, and must have required a vast expenditure of labour. Hundreds of thousands of pine-trees, from eight inches to one foot in thickness, have been laid transversely upon each other, and filled in with rammed earth, the causeway being deeply ditched on each side. The Chickahominy at this point can scarcely be called a river; it is a succession of winding streams, isles, and swamps, requiring a bridge some five hundred yards in length to span it. The same engineering corps has the credit of the erection, and a more solidly constructed affair I never walked over. As we approached the head of the bridge, a signboard on a huge oak-tree informed us it was constructed by the New York Engineer Brigade in five days, the information being prefaced with the notice, 'The Road to Richmond.' The country on the other side rose rapidly, and was covered with our encampments as far as the eye could reach—not very far, however, for the open stands merely in the proportion of one to two of forest and wood. A walk of two miles brought us to our present camping ground, Fair Oaks, close to the railroad, and within a few minutes' march of the battle-fields of May 31st and June 1st; and a more execrable camping ground I have not seen in all my campaigning experience.

The country beyond the Chickahominy is even more hilly than to the northward, and incomparably more swampy. I can imagine no worse locality for health than the region now occupied by the Army of the Potomac, and easily understand why Virginians, when wishing to describe any region as particularly unhealthy, always compare it to the swamps of the Chickahominy. Swamp, swamp everywhere, on the tops and slopes of the hills, and covering the valleys—dry now in some places, but only to throw off deadliest miasma. To make matters worse, there are upwards of a hundred thousand men occupying every foot of ground, hiding their tents in the trees, camping in the hollows, and spreading acres of canvas over the hill-sides. Thousands of horses still further poison the soil; and space, in fine, is so limited, that garbage and all else must lie where it falls, fermenting and steaming in the sun's rays. We are in the shadow of an upas forest, and within a stone's throw rest the half-buried corpses of the many slain in the two days' action of Fair Oaks, and the offal of hecatombs of oxen impossible to cart away. This foul stratum of decaying animal and vegetable matter is washed through by the rains, and becomes more dangerous than ever to life when mixed with the poisonous mud. The water is awful: at one camp it is blue, at another green, changing elsewhere to brown, yellow, or some other tint, but always opaque, odorous, and disgusting. Smells! I am tired of trying to count their number: Cologne is a perfumer's shop compared to this peninsula, and yet here we must remain until the moment comes for us to move. When that will be, nobody pretends to say; but it must be a very near period, or the army will be destroyed. I hear dreadful reports of the general health—reports which are not permitted to find publicity in the Northern press. One brigade arrived here a month ago 5,000 strong; it cannot now take 2,200 into the field; and from all I can gather, regiments originally 1,000 strong do not now average half that number. Our brigade has only been here twenty-four hours, but the miasma is already beginning to tell upon us, and several of our officers are apparently sickening for typhoid or intermittent. McClellan must indeed move soon, or half his army will have to nurse or bury the other half.

Franklin's and Porter's *corps d'armée* hitherto have camped in comparatively healthy localities, but still very unhealthy in comparison with Northern Virginia. During the past fortnight this has especially been the case, deaths being frequent and sick lists continually on the increase. If I have kept my health, it is simply by avoiding water as much as possible, exposure still more so, and by thoroughly saturating the system with quinine. The alternative is not pleasant, but I hope by the end of the campaign to regard the sulphate as a luxury. Perhaps, even, I may become enthusiastic about it! *Quien sabe?* The really warm weather is only just commencing, and I shudder to think what a pest-heap this peninsula will be after the collision of these two enormous armies. There is really not sufficient room to fight in here, and the slaughter will be frightful: the fronts of the rival armies are within half-a-mile of each other, and the pickets are so close that a general action may be brought about at any moment. Shells are bursting continually through the day and occasionally at night, and we are becoming so accustomed to the reports as to pay little attention to them.

McClellan's lines extend from Newbridge on the Chickahominy to Fair Oaks on the York River Railroad, thence to the western edge of White Oak Swamp on the Charles City pike-road—a distance of about six miles. Heintzelman holds the left, Keyes and Sumner the centre, and Franklin and Porter's corps form the right wing. I hear that Heintzelman is in communication with the gunboats on the James River, but how he manages it I know not.

An immense amount of work has been accomplished by this army since its arrival in the peninsula; many miles of substantial corduroyed roads run in all directions, and the telegraph wire interlaces the different camps. I hope to visit the works in front to-morrow.

June 21.

Heavy dew fell last night, and the sun was oppressively hot by eight o'clock this morning—too hot, in fact, for anyone to remain under its rays with any regard to his safety. Canvas tents are but a slight protection, even with the sides looped up all round, and the insect world is more numerous in the midst of these swamps than imagination can depict. As I write, enormous ants attempt to run over my paper, beetles of all dimensions perform their gymnastics on my clothes, and flies plague me with their bites, which both tickle and irritate. We cannot help the matter by grumbling; their attentions must be borne, for they are the courtiers and retinue of Queen Cloacina, who holds her court in these swamps.

Our camp is situated on the north side of the Richmond and West Point Railroad, close to the station called Fair Oaks. Between us and the railroad lies the scene of the battle of the 31st May, at only five minutes' walk from our encampment. Shakespeare's blasted heath was not so appalling, for it wanted the parching sun, the death-teeming dust, and the wreck of battle. Macbeth's witches would have chosen this spot as a summer resort, and I almost believed I saw them hovering over the scene this morning in the guise of turkey-buzzards attracted by the scent of offal. Can your fancy depict an immense expanse of yellow mud, dried and fetid, erst the locality of a forest, where giant oaks and towering pines wooed the traveller to quiet shades? There, the former abode of peace and beauty, we now see but a horrible desert, parched and dry, stumps of trees bristling the expanse, trunks blackened with fire! Strew amidst these ten thousand faggots embedded in earth, the remains of clothing—caps, boots, shoes, shirts, blankets, pools of stagnant water, broken arms, rations—food for maggots, horrid grinning heads of oxen, hides mosaic'd into earth by rains, mounds covering the plain, beneath which lie the remains of human-kind; bodies of gallant men, friend and foe, with a few inches of dust over them, and feet and hands here and there cropping out from their last resting-place. Boom! boom! The ear is startled with the report of cannon near by. The shells come shrieking towards you, and explosions are heard in the woods bounding this mighty tomb. A rush of air in front of you, and myriads of flies darken your sight as you tread upon their banquet of putrescent vileness; the nostrils become filled with odours too foul as your foot slips upon the carrion grease, and you run, heart-sick, into the sheltering grove. Every sense is active in this realm of indescribable horrors!

Five minutes' walk brought me to the front of our lines, where a far-extending earthwork--breast-high in some places, mounted with guns in others—forbade farther advance. Our pickets are thrown forward into the woods some three hundred yards, and it is easy to see that the whole of this army will have to devote itself to bush-fighting over several miles before reaching the open ground which is said to surround Richmond. Redoubts are thick as bristles on a brush, but they are in every case mounted with field-guns. I have not seen, nor can I hear, of a single siege-piece, although some persons who ought to know assert that a heavy siege-train is on its way here. The troops are now building corduroy roads through the woods to enable the artillery to reach the open, and desultory firing contines along the entire line.

McClellan has just passed to the front. I must conclude this letter in order to see what his visit portends, particularly as we hear of a fight in prospect on the extreme right of our line.

CAMP LINCOLN, FAIR OAKS, NEAR RICHMOND: June 23.

Camp Lincoln is the official title of General McClellan's head-quarters this side of the Chickahominy; and although our camp is a mile removed from that point, the whole of Franklin's *corps d'armée* is assumed to be within the same lines. Probably Fitz-John Porter's command will likewise be included when it crosses the river.

Smith's and Slocum's divisions, composing Franklin's corps, are encamped in an immense irregular open space —a Virginia wheat field, in fine, for that is the only term which can describe the vast plains under culture in this State. The west side of this plain is bounded by a broad strip of woods, a road following the sinuosities of the forest edge, and our troops have been engaged since their arrival in improving the route by corduroying it along its entire extent. Such labour is indeed required, for no amount of hot weather seems capable of drying this land or divesting it of its springiness. The surface may be cracked, and shoals of dust may cloud the view, but the foot of the pedestrian sinks nevertheless, and a few inches bring you to water. Infantry can get along without much difficulty, but cavalry must walk leisurely, whilst wagons, and above all, artillery, stick fast continually. Six hours' rain would render the roads here impassable, and it has therefore become a matter of necessity to corduroy them before any offensive movement can be made. The operation is effected in the following manner: pine trunks, a foot thick, are first laid across the route; similar sticks are then placed across them longitudinally, and these latter carry the roadway composed of logs eight inches in diameter.

Ditches two feet deep bound the road on either side, and the probabilities are that the route will remain hard and firm under any continuance of wet weather; surely it ought to do so with nearly a yard thick of green timber. Branch roads strike off towards the great front through the woods, all similarly constructed, and although tens of thousands of trees have been felled and trimmed for the purpose, yet there seems to be small diminution in the forests. If Virginia gains nothing else from this war she will, at all events, possess at its close what she never possessed before—admirable means of intercommunication.

Four hours' walk yesterday morning along the front gave no evidence whatever of siege works; there is plenty of artillery—10-pounder rifled pieces, and 18, 24 and 32-pounder howitzers mounted in position. The construction of the numerous roads above referred to is absolutely necessary in order to use artillery. At the battle of West Point the rebels were unable to bring any guns to bear upon Franklin's division, and they were in like predicament in the first day's battle of Fair Oaks on the 31st of May. At this battle of Fair Oaks they captured all Casey's batteries from him, and turned them upon the Federals; this was affected at the very commencement of the action, before the infantry could arm themselves to defend their artillery. It was a surprise well conceived and admirably well executed, but such an one as will not occur again. Casey's division is now in the rear of Kearny's, and Kearny is a man who pickets a mile farther out than his orders absolutely require, whilst he himself passes most of his time among his pickets.

Crossing the belt of woods dividing our encampment from the front, the scene is full of activity and life. Here and there small camps nestle in the shade of magnificent trees—they are the head-quarters of brigade generals; thousand of horses belonging to mounted officers and the artillery find shelter from the sun's rays, and details of men are engaged in felling lofty pines and preparing them for roadways. Outside the wood we come upon another far-reaching plain, stockaded, as it were, with stumps, rendering progress difficult. Scores of canvas camps vary the landscape, some of them shaded with branches of trees—green no longer, for their luxuriance has long since borne the deathliness of autumn. Dust and smoke from the cook-fires blind the eyes, and open spaces are blackened by the charred remains of former encampments. Yet is the scene not devoid of beauty, for we stand on the crest of a chain of hills, and the principal valley of the Chickahominy lies beneath us on the right, forests rising above each other in the distance, with the camp of Porter's corps perched seemingly in the very trees. Copses, richly green, dot the valley, pale wreaths of smoke marking the posts of pickets, and the occasional gleam of a bayonet warning the careless pedestrian. A quarter of a mile across the open in front of us stretches a narrow belt of trees with thick tangled bushes around their stems. Before reaching them, however, we must traverse a deep ravine, and it is a matter of astonishment to me that the enemy have not thought proper to hold such an admirable defensive position. A muddy, fetid swamp lies in the bottom—we have spanned it with a substantial artillery bridge—and we mount the farther side by climbing rather than walking. A few more yards of open, and we enter the woods; small but steep hills covered with bushes hide our pickets, and a strong line of skirmishers are ever on the *qui vive* in the wheat and oat fields beyond.

About due west from our encampment, and within half

a mile from where I am writing, there is a high hill; upon its near base watch these skirmishers, the enemy's pickets being only two hundred yards in front of them. A slim belt of trees crowns the summit of this eminence, the intervening space being covered with oats breast-high, fast ripening under the fierce Virginia sun. Far as the eye can reach to the left, blue-coated soldiers stand apart, some trailing their arms, others leaning on the muzzles of their rifles, all gazing watchfully, earnestly, into the woods beyond. A man steps out from behind a tree across the fields, and the bluecoats grasp their muskets, straitening ready to fire; half a dozen murky-grey suits join the man from the edge of the copse, and our side of the field becomes a wall of skirmishers, almost shoulder to shoulder. But none fire. It is the day of rest, and loyal and rebel have tacitly agreed to respect the holy Sabbath.

This hill will probably, ere long, be the scene of fierce conflict. General McClellan is stated to have declared that his artillery once upon its summit, Richmond is his; if so, why does he not endeavour to obtain possession of it? General Franklin, and others in whom he is known to place confidence, have crept forwards on their hands and feet through the oats, and reconnoitred the country beyond, and it is easy to discover, without going so far as they did, that an immense plain—perhaps half a mile wide—descends gradually on the other side towards the doomed city. The *élite* of the army of the Potomac front the position—40,000 of McClellan's picked troops are within a dash of it; and thirty batteries of field artillery (including the reserve, some of the batteries being twenty and thirty-pounder rifled guns) may approach to the very base of the hill without the knowledge of the enemy. Our corduroyed roads converge towards this point, and the impression is general throughout the right wing that our first attack will be made here. The Confederates, I judge, are not ignorant of the value of this natural 'Malakoff;' partially hidden by the wall of trees on the crest, I discern with my field-glass a peaceful farm-house; the lower windows and the door are not visible, nor indeed much of the upper story, for a yellow-looking wall tells plainly of an earthwork upon which guns will bristle when they are wanted. Farther to the right, and a little to the rear, I catch sight of several roofs, and here I am informed the enemy have a strong redoubt, but I am too far down the decline to discern the works.

Having thus visited the point which we now speak of as 'the hill,' I turn my steps backwards towards our lines, availing myself as much as possible of the forest shade. Everything is quiet; but I mark that strong arms have lately been at work in these pine groves, trunks of equal length and thickness lying around in heaps, while in one spot I find two solid bridges ready to span some ravine or marsh. The click of the axe and the deep 'thud' of the fallen tree will echo again through the forest to-morrow; and woods and glades and gurgling rivulets calmly reposing in the rest of the Sabbath, tenanted now by sweet-throated birds and brilliant butterflies, will awake again to the voice of the soldier woodsman, and the sharp report of the death-carrying rifle.

One long continuous breastwork runs the entire length of our lines, at some thirty paces from the edge of the forest; underneath the trees are pitched the little shelter-tents (*tentes d'abri*) of the troops, and the arms are stacked ready for immediate action in the roadway in front. I walked for three miles yesterday between this *cheveux de frise* of glistening bayonets and the interminable breastwork built up on the inside with pine logs, and affording an admiable protection to infantry. At different points, so as to command the woods beyond, there are detached works, lunettes, demilunes, &c., mounted with from two to six guns, all field-pieces. I saw no preparations whatever for siege artillery, notwithstanding the report that such is on its way here; but it is of course easy to mount heavy guns on the works, should such be required. Indeed, some parties venture to assert that the same plan will be adopted here as at Corinth and Yorktown—namely, regular approaches; if so, and Heaven forfend, we must linger out our patience during the summer months in this vile swamp region of the Chickahominy, with the almost certainty that so soon as our preparations are complete, the enemy will change their front, and render our works useless. The partisans of General McClellan assure us that his policy of persistent *inertia* is a mark of profound strategy; that he has thereby saved Washington from attack and transferred the seat of war from Northern to Southern Virginia. In the opinion of dull-headed mortals, not blessed with genius or blind appreciation, the time is drawing nigh for the display of a little activity—unless the contest is to be decided by simple endurance. Since the evacuation of Yorktown, seven weeks ago, we have lost upwards of 40,000 men from this army *by sickness and desertion alone.* The fact is, of course, kept as secret as possible, but you will hear it so asserted daily, especially by those officers who are especially qualified to speak on the subject—the army surgeons. The major portion of this enormous loss is placed to the account of desertion—by some, be it understood, but not by the majority, for they know better, to their own cost. How, in the name of all that is reasonable, could men desert in numbers equal to a large army, and we know nothing of it? The Southern papers claim no such loss to our ranks, and it would be egregious to imagine 40,000 men skulking off to the North, *a distance, in a direct line, of* 150 *miles,* without let or hindrance. If desertion be the true cause of this tremendous depletion in our ranks, McClellan ought to be court-martialed for incompetency, or worse; but it is sickness, and sickness alone, playing the game of the Southern generals, and yet our army is constantly being crowded into narrower limits, as though with a foregone conclusion to submit us to the teeming horrors of these malarious swamps. How men can continue to profess confidence in such leadership is a mystery; yet we are assured by certain newspapers and officers of high rank, that McClellan's plans for this campaign were all matured in the spring, and that a blow was to be struck on the left flank of the rebel army at Manasses which would have cut off its railroad communications with the West. General Joseph Johnston saw through this at the eleventh hour, say they, and avoided the danger by evacuating his works. The same thing occurred at Yorktown, rendering McClellan's magnificent lines of fortifications totally useless; and after Halleck had expended weeks in investing Corinth, Beauregard slipped away quietly with all his army, artillery, and stores. We are thus led to judge what is the general plan of the enemy in dealing with the invaders—a Fabian policy, in fine, like McClellan's; but it is doubtful whether a Fabian policy will tend so much to the advantage of the attacking party as to the weaker one defending its soil. Will the results be the same here in front of Richmond? I do not pretend to express any opinion on that point, but officers of this army, from commanders of divisions to companies, are beginning to grumble at the delay, and secretly express the conviction that something is wrong. You will have seen in the Northern papers that Fremont is retreating northward, down the Valley of the Shenandoah, in consequence of Stonewall Jackson having been newly reinforced by 12,000 men. This looks to many as though the Confederates were preparing to transfer their force to the hilly regions of Western Virginia, where immense supplies of grain and provisions will enable them to continue the contest throughout the summer, holding at the same time the line of the Kanawha Canal, between Richmond, Lynchburg, and the Valley. It would take many a long and weary month to beat them out of that region, vastly stronger as it is, strategetically, than any they have yet taken up.

June 24.

The extraordinary silence of the enemy on Sunday and during the morning and afternoon of yesterday induced the generals on the left and centre of our line to throw forward their pickets. Half a mile in advance they came upon the rebel's pickets, whom they drove back; but these latter being supported by their reserves, our men had to retreat in turn, followed up sharply by the enemy. The Confederate troops marched boldly out of the woods to within some three hundred yards of our entrenchments, when a brisk shelling from our batteries compelled them to retire in haste. An hour before sunset is usually the time for the enemy to break silence, and scarcely a day passes without our being regaled with heavy musketry and cannonading towards evening. It was so on Saturday night, and the conflict was so well sustained from the commencement that all the troops along our line were ordered under arms with the expectation of repelling a general attack on our works. Before sunrise this morning the attack was renewed at the south point—that portion of the line between Fair-Oaks and Seven Pines—and the army was immediately ready to start in light marching order with three days' rations. The firing has ceased, however, and the troops have returned to their usual avocation—universal digging.

It would now seem that we are to approach Richmond by a regular siege. Several facts prove this, and we may therefore make up our minds for occupying these swamps during the hottest portion of the summer. A walk this morning to the Fair Oaks station of the railroad through our camps enabled me to see a number of siege pieces waiting removal to the line, and I have since learned that several are already in position at the front. The eternal spade, too, is more active than ever in both armies; redoubts are being thrown up daily, I might almost say; and within a short period every little eminence will be capped with a battery.

I cannot see how M‘Clellan's hesitation is to be accounted for: he has all the troops now that he can expect; his roads are complete, and a large fleet of gunboats lies in the James River, awaiting his orders to attack the rebel batteries. The only movements made suggest an occupation of this position during a considerable period, certainly no offensive operations. General Casey is ordered with his division to Whitehouse, on the Pamunkey, evidently to protect our basis of supply from such attacks as that made by Stuart's cavalry a fortnight ago; and I am also informed that the Prince de Joinville, the Comte de Paris, and Duc de Chartres are about to quit the army in order to return to Europe. It was originally their intention to accompany General McClellan as far as the city of Richmond, and if they now change their determination it is probably because events are transpiring which will prevent our march on that capital.

CHAPTER XIX.

THE RETREAT.

June 25 (10 P.M.).

We have had a brisk artillery fight along the lines to-day, but it was at first difficult to understand whether we or the enemy were the aggressors. As soon as it became evident that something more than usual was on the programme, I hastened to that portion of our lines resting on the south bank of the Chickahominy, whence the most extended view is to be obtained, and found our artillery in great force on the summit of the hills, but not as yet engaged. The ground held by us in this locality is admirably suited for holding. An elevated *plateau* covered with strong redoubts, the ridge lined with breastworks of solid construction and most difficult of approach, is fronted by a lengthy expanse of open till it descends finally into the valley. The only fault one could find with the position, is that of its being thoroughly commanded by the heights of Gaines' Mills, north of the river; so that if FitzJohn Porter should be driven from his works, we should be compelled to evacuate ours, and—' skedaddle' at double-quick. For the which reason, it appears to me that some of the regiments here encamped would be much better placed on the north side the Chickahominy.

Hearing on the right that Hooker and Kearny were engaging the enemy on our left, I started along the front towards the railroad, and discovered that the entire army was under arms. Having proceeded as far as the old battle-field of Fair Oaks, the sound of musketry became distinct and rapid, and I could occasionally hear the *staccato* 'hurrah' of the Union troops, and the peculiar continuous cheer of the rebels. The puffs of white smoke hanging in the woods told indubitably of shells, and I was advised by a quiet old major to continue my walk rather more from the front than the previous portion of my promenade. Shell and round shot are very demoralising to those unaccustomed to them; but after a few weeks' active campaigning, one begins to understand that artillery is not so terrible as it pretends to be, coming somewhat under the category of moral suasion. But when you hear the angry, rapid crackling of musketry, look out! I continued my walk through the woods backing our front, and found regiment after regiment waiting in the shade for orders to advance, and all anxious to get at the enemy. A mile from the railway, I reached the rear of Heintzelman's lines, and found the wounded being rapidly brought in from the front; everybody seemed in high spirits at the progress of the day's work, and word was passed along the lines that Hooker was driving the enemy, and had already gained half a mile of ground. While pushing my investigations in this quarter, the thunder of artillery broke out loudly in the direction of the river, seeming to come from the very point I had left an hour or two previously: believing that Franklin's corps was at length getting into action, and the ground held by him being much better suited for watching the ebb and flow of battle, I bent my steps homeward. The cannonading grew more distinct and rapid as I progressed; but before I reached camp, I discovered that it arose from the lines at Mechanicsville, General M'Call and the enemy being actively engaged. At this hour, we are given to understand that Hooker has gained an important advantage on our left wing, holding all the ground covered by his advance in the morning; while M'Call has been enjoying nothing further than artillery practice, although the enemy have shown themselves in great masses towards the Virginia Central Road. We are ordered to be under arms at daybreak, and confidently expect hot work to-morrow. I hope, however, that' the thermometer will not stand at 97° in the shade, as it has done to-day.

June 29.

The events of the past four days have been too numerous and exciting for the most cold-blooded mortal to diarise them as they occurred. My narrative must continue by the help of the few jottings I have been able to make *running*, and with the aid of memory. The brain has been so much on the stretch since Wednesday last, that I feel confident none of the details of the past four days will ever escape my remembrance.

I write sitting on a beautiful grassy hill south of White Oak Swamp, and close to White Oak Creek, where it is crossed by the bridge leading to the Long Bridge Road. It is a beautiful Sunday morning: regiments are hurrying across the deep creek with the greatest rapidity, and hastening with the utmost speed to M'Clellan's new base—the James River. All our labours on that dreary peninsula have gone for nothing, but nobody regrets leaving it for a healthier locality. I wish, however, that our change of base had a little less appearance of being compulsory.

How I managed to get here safely, Heaven alone knows! But I must not anticipate.

About noon of Thursday (June 26th), M'Call was

attacked in force at Mechanicsville by enormous masses of the enemy. So it was reported on our own part of the lines, and the fact was plainly correct, as our corps rested upon its arms anxiously expecting the order to advance to his support. At night-time the noise in the direction of our right front entirely subsided, and we learned that M'Call had gallantly repulsed every attack and still held his works at Mechanicsville. Our troops were in glorious spirits at the news, and the enthusiasm was further increased when the order came from head-quarters for the bands to play. Our musicians had led an absolutely idle life since leaving White House, and it was pleasant to hear them once again, and the stentorian cheers of the soldiers fading away in the far distance. We little imagined what was threatening us on the morrow.

The enemy's attack upon M'Call was an admirably-planned movement to get the mass of their forces in that general's rear, between Mechanicsville and the Pamunkey. Lee evidently shifted his head-quarters to some purpose; and it is a matter of astonishment to me, as to others, that M°Clellan also shifted his to south of the river about the very time deserters reported to us that his shrewd antagonist was massing his forces so as to threaten our right flank. While it was obvious to everybody who visited Mechanicsville that the rebels have for two or three weeks past been increasing their camps in that direction, we have been diminishing our forces north of the Chickahominy by transferring Franklin's corps to the southern bank, leaving Porter's corps and M'Call's division to breast the flood alone. Since last Wednesday there have been camp rumours of changing our base, so that our present advance to the James may be in accordance with a long-settled plan on the part of M°Clellan; but it certainly does seem strange that the movement could not be effected without such terrible fighting and bloodshed as we have experienced since Thursday. At an early hour on Friday morning, M'Call discovered that the enemy was in overwhelming force on his right flank and rear; and he fell back as rapidly as possible to FitzJohn Porter's lines at Gaines' Mills. The foe advanced towards the latter position with the utmost rapidity, and the action commenced soon after noon. I lay sick in camp that day, suffering from intermittent neuralgia, the regimental surgeon assuring me that if I exposed myself to the sun, *typhoid* might be a very probable result. The order came about two o'clock for the 1st Jersey Brigade to cross the Chickahominy to reinforce Porter. Colonel Torbert, of the 1st Regiment, was sick like myself, and we kept each other company in his tent listening to the combat raging furiously on our right. The colonel did not believe that the brigade, after all, would get into action, so many false alarms had we been the victims of during the campaign; but he made his officers promise, that if this time should prove an exception, they would immediately send for him. An hour and a half later, an orderly rode full tilt into the deserted camp, bringing word that the brigade was engaged, and the young colonel, so weak from fever that he could scarcely get to the tent-door, forthwith mounted his horse and rode off. Some ten minutes after his departure, Meagher's Irish Brigade marched past our camp in the direction of the fight: when the rear ranks disappeared in the woods, I again lay down on the blankets, and slept soundly for the first time in twenty-four hours. It was six o'clock when the colonel's old negro-servant, Ananias, came and shook me roughly, saying, 'Look here, sir, you've got to clear out of this, for the rebs are shelling our camp.' I got up immediately, and found there was no mistake about it, for the shells were bursting in dangerous proximity all around. It took me but a few minutes to put on what was necessary, resolving, during the operation, to seek M°Clellan's head-quarters. Leaving the tent, I asked Ananias where he was going, when he replied curtly, 'Why, I'm gwine to stay here: I'be got nuffin to do with this fight.' (The President's proclamation of emancipation had not then been issued.)

I made the best of my way through the woods to M°Clellan's head-quarters, every step seeming to take me further from the scene of action, although I could occasionally hear shells bursting and crashing in the woods about me. The general's head-quarters were in an open plain, and I must own to some astonishment at hearing he was in his tent, instead of being with his troops at Gaines' Mills. Running against an acquaintance belonging to the staff, I accepted his hospitality for the night, and soon learned that FitzJohn Porter was crossing the river to our side, the enemy being in such overwhelming numbers that he could not retain his position. I saw by the faces of all about me that we were getting the worst of it, but to what extent I could only surmise. Early yesterday morning, I learned that the general's head-quarters were to be transferred to Savage's Station, and I proceeded in that direction immediately after breakfast, reaching the spot fixed on for the encampment with the head-quarters train. Towards three o'clock, hundreds of wounded were brought in and laid in the numerous hospital tents, and, when these were full, on the ground. The enemy was evidently following up our retreating army with terrible rapidity; they had crossed the river, and the wounded of our rear guard were already reaching us. While helping these poor suffering fellows

o

by what means were in my power, I saw a tall, sedate civilian, apparently of fifty years, strolling through the hospital grounds, aiding the surgeons, and occasionally helping a wounded soldier from an ambulance. Few there knew it was the Prince de Joinville. I watched him at his labours for upwards of an hour, filling this man's canteen with cool water, or bringing fresh lint to another, whose arm or leg he would tend with the carefulness of a woman.

Heintzelman's head-quarters were close to this hospital. I called upon the gruff old general on leaving the latter, and chatted with him at his tent-door for some ten minutes. Whilst we were comparing notes, his quartermaster came up and asked what were the orders in regard to baggage. 'Everything to be destroyed,' said the general. 'The officers' bedding too?' was the reply. 'Yes, sir,' answered Heintzelman; 'the general's orders are that everything not absolutely necessary must be left behind; so pitch everybody's private traps out of your waggons.' I knew better than to ask questions, but it began to look to me like a retreat in downright good earnest, not a mere 'change of base.'

Back again to head-quarters, where I learned that M°Clellan's private waggon train would cross White Oak Swamp during the night. I was offered for my own personal convenience a light buggy—one of those slight-looking American traps, in which, they say, 'a horse can trot 2.40 without knowing he'd got anything behind him'—about as unreasonable an affair for campaigning as ever was looked upon. I accepted *avec empressement*, being assured the coloured boy was very careful, and 'would take me through all safe.' We started with the waggons as it was getting dusk, and about nine o'clock entered the northern end of the swamp. The huge, dense trees made the night dark as Erebus, open spaces occasionally giving us a momentary glimpse of the road. Hundreds of waggons wended their way through the seemingly interminable forest, whole regiments of infantry with now and then a troop of cavalry passed us, until the darkness and monotony of the journey sent me to sleep. How long I slept I know not, but at last—CRASH! I found myself on the ground under the feet of horses, loud cries of demoralised teamsters sounding around me. I got out of danger with a leap, and then discovered that my frail vehicle had been run into down-hill by an army waggon, the buggy smashed literally in pieces, and the negro-boy *non est inventus*. He too, however, was unhurt. I was then offered a seat in General Van Vliet's army carriage, the very one in which the wife of General Lee had been conducted outside our lines, and slept comfortably until five o'clock this morning, when we reached the edge of the swamp, and rejoiced at finding ourselves in the open country.

On the hills, where I am now writing, the rebels, in months gone by, have thrown up long lines of earthworks and redoubts. Luckily for us, they were unoccupied; for had there been a single division holding the works, we could never have crossed the broad and deep creek, and we should all have been captured or destroyed in that horrible White Oak Swamp.*

HAXALL's FARM, TURKEY BEND, JAMES RIVER :
July 1 (10 P.M.).

By dint of no small running and hard fighting, the Army of the Potomac has had the good luck to reach the James

---

* Magruder, or Huger, had received orders from General Lee to advance rapidly and occupy these works, but failed to do so. Had the orders been carried out as intended, there would have been an end of the Army of the Potomac.

River; and, if report be correct, we have also saved the major portion of our waggon trains, although many pieces of artillery have been lost or captured. We had a good two hours' start of the enemy, and have certainly proved the truth of the maxim, that 'a stern chase is a long one.' A retreating army has great advantages over a pursuer, notably in the choice of ground for turning upon its enemy; and the country through which we have passed is admirably adapted for defensive operations.

The army was not clear of White Oak Swamp until Monday,—Heintzelman's divisions, under Kearny and Hooker, bringing up the rear. These two generals have performed the major portion of the fighting on the Peninsula since the evacuation of Yorktown, and their determined attitude and the dauntless bravery of their troops kept the victorious rebels at respectful distance during our retreat, and enabled the entire army to reach its present position on the James.

FitzJohn Porter's corps led our advance, striking for the Quaker Road. The latter runs from Charles City Cross Roads, over Malvern Hills, to the Newmarket Road, and, once in our possession, we should be safe, and within easy distance of the river and the gunboats. After crossing White Oak Swamp, I resolved to attach myself to Fitz-John Porter's command, and was then made aware, for the first time during the campaign, what a number of cavalry regiments McClellan has in his army. For the first time, too, they have been made some use of—scouting in force between our advance and the river, directing the infantry where to take up position, and pointing out the roads for the teamsters to follow.

The march of the past two days was comparatively barren of incident to myself, although very exciting. Retreating

in an enemy's country, with a determined foe hanging on
your rear and flank, is by no means conducive to a proper
mental equilibrium, especially when your road lies through
woods and hills and narrow lanes, where a well-posted regiment might keep an army at bay for hours. We were constantly the victims of scares; the cavalry coming in full tilt
with reports of the enemy appearing in this or that locality.
Above the trees in our rear we could occasionally see the
smoke of battle, and hear the reverberation of artillery.
But we reached Malvern Hills this morning without
difficulty, and the different regiments as they debouched
from the forest were immediately drawn up in line of
battle. The early morning was frightfully hot, and as we
were now clear of the woods, and were marching on the
enormous wheat-fields belonging to Haxall's plantation,
we got the full benefit of the sun's rays. I saw many a
poor fellow drop down from sunstroke; and to prevent
trouble to myself from what threatened, I saturated my
broad-brimmed slouch-hat with water, and kept it constantly
wet during the day. The splendid wheat grown on this
far-famed plantation—short in the straw, the grain small,
round, and delicious in flavour—was still uncut, and the
troops, as they marched through it to take up their
appointed positions, stuffed their pockets and knapsacks
with the ripe ears. The view from the summit of these
far-stretching hills was beautiful in the extreme; the country fell away from us for miles, and we could see the goal
of our hopes—the James River—sparkling refreshingly
in the distant valley. While the troops were lying under
arms in the blazing sun, the thousands of waggons de-
scended the hills on the southern slope, making for the
neighbourhood of the river by a road which soon became
lost to our sight in the dense forests. But we could still

trace its course for miles by the sinuous clouds of yellow dust which rose above the trees.

After some enquiry, I learned that McClellan's head-quarters were on the banks of the river, at Haxall's residence, where I am now writing. Since leaving Savage's Station last Saturday, I have not had my boots or clothes off me; and I started immediately at a quick pace for the point in question, full of hope for a thorough wash and shaking the dust out of my clothes. After a three miles' walk through interminable lines of army waggons, I reached the house, and found a number of navy and army officers on the lawn around it—among them my old friend Captain John Rodgers, of the iron-clad 'Galena,' who was in command of the gun-boat squadron in the river. He gave me an invitation to board his vessel, which, I need scarcely say, I gladly accepted; for I have only had two meals since Saturday, keeping body and soul together with excitement and Indian corn whiskey—when I had the luck to get it. About twenty minutes subsequent to the captain's invitation, there was a cloud of dust in the road, and General McClellan entered the garden, accompanied by the French Princes and other officers of his staff. The arrival, so far as I was concerned, was not fortunate. Captain Rodgers came to me shortly after, and stated that inasmuch as the general was coming immediately on board the 'Galena,' it would be better for me to postpone my visit. I saw him put off in the captain's boat with a heavy heart, and he remained on the vessel until evening.

During the previous hour, there had been rapid artillery fire in the direction of Malvern Hills, and reports from the front soon made it apparent that a severe battle was in progress. I went down to the river washing the shores of the garden, and enjoyed a bathe as never before. Half a mile up the stream, the 'Galena' and her consorts were furiously shelling the heights on the northern bank; army signal officers being stationed in line from the scene of action to the river, and giving directions where to fire the shell. Hundreds of men were swimming and washing in the stream, and the whole scene was about as strange and inspiring as one could imagine.

Feeling somewhat more comfortable and comparatively braced up, I started towards evening for the battle-field, which, however, I did not reach. At the foot of the hills, I learned that the battle was already won, and that the army would shortly take up its march in our direction. The action was represented to me as by far the most severe fought on the Peninsula; but nobody could tell who was in command of our troops. When I stated that General M'Clellan was on board the 'Galena' in the river, few would believe me, and one officer told me to my face it was a d—d lie: if he follow the advice I gave, his enquiries will satisfy him that my statement was correct. When I again reached head-quarters, I found the garden of the house encumbered with wounded officers, and General M Clellan still on board the 'Galena.' I met him coming ashore half an hour after my return, and he immediately left for the battle-field, where he still is, I presume.

Everybody seems to think that we are to hold this position as our new base of operations against Richmond, and it is satisfactory to learn that large reinforcements are already arriving from Fortress Monroe by way of the James River. But if we failed to take the rebel capital after lying within five miles of it during a whole month, how long shall we require when our lines are four times that distance? Matters certainly look very much 'mixed up.'

HARRISON'S LANDING: July 2.

We have changed our base to six miles farther from Richmond, and the whole army is making its way back from Malvern Hills in a shocking state of demoralisation. Except in a few commands, regimental and other organisations are completely broken up, and men are endeavouring to find brigades and divisions which appear no longer to exist.

The hot weather changed last night to rain, but rain in torrents. We are now encamped in one vast mud puddle, where it is all but impossible for men to walk, and horses and waggons stick powerless. If the enemy attack us here, it is difficult to tell what can save us.

July 3 (11 A.M.).

The army is to be re-organised before undertaking further operations. This will be a work of many weeks, and all those whose duties do not necessitate their remaining here are talking of going north. Several transports go down the river this afternoon, and I have obtained a pass to return in one of them to Fortress Monroe.

CONCLUSION.

When the history of the Slaveholders' Rebellion shall be written, Major-General McClellan will hold a foremost place in its pages. His merits as a commander will then be decided by his management of the campaign on the Yorktown Peninsula, and the historian must then answer these questions:—

1.—With the means at his command and his universally conceded superiority in numbers, was it a proof of skill on his part to permit the Confederate army to remain within sight of Washington during upwards of six months without a single attempt to dislodge them?

2.—Is not ample evidence forthcoming that when the two advance *corps* of the Army of the Potomac arrived on the Peninsula, the Confederates were so little prepared for their approach that Yorktown might have been taken by a *coup de main* with but slight opposition?

3.—Had General McClellan been present on the field of Williamsburg during the action of May 5th, thus insuring accord amongst his subordinates, is it not probable that the repulse of the Confederate army would have been turned into a total rout?

4.—When the Confederate army retreated up the Peninsula and across the Chickahominy, was there any reason whatever why McClellan should not have immediately followed it over that stream?

5.—Was it not an unpardonable blunder to divide his army in twain by a river which might at any period become so swollen as to render one portion of his command utterly powerless to assist the other?

6.—Did he display common foresight, humanity, or generalship in drawing his lines around the city of Richmond in a region notorious throughout his country as one of the most unhealthy of the South?

7.—Were his enormous parks of artillery of any service to him throughout the campaign?

8.—Did he make use of his cavalry, except during the retreat?

9.—Commencing with the battle of Williamsburg—the first on the Peninsula, and closing with the last—that of Malvern Hills, did not General McClellan persistently imperil the safety of his army by leaving the conduct of the several actions to his subordinates, never appearing on the field until the close of the engagement?

10.—In discussing the question whether General McClellan were properly reinforced by the War Department, will it not be necessary first to enquire whether he made good and sufficient use of the means already at his disposal?

11.—Did General McClellan use the Army of the Potomac as a weapon with which to crush the enemies of the Union, or as a tool wherewith to build up a sectional political party, thereby seeking his own personal advantage?

Whatever answers shall be given to these questions, it must at all events be conceded that the campaign on the Yorktown Peninsula was the first great effort of the North to deal seriously with the Rebellion. The preparations extended over many months; and when General McClellan led his divisions to the banks of the Chickahominy, he could pride himself upon being at the head of an army as numerous, and incomparably better armed and equipped than any of modern times.

He failed lamentably in achieving aught but disaster, and by sheer chance alone was his army saved from annihilation. To what cause history will ascribe his failure—whether to incompetency, want of energy and courage, or disbelief in his country's destiny—I say not; but it never will be said that means were not placed at his disposal sufficient to command success, had he but possessed the ability and patriotism of other American commanders.

The world never believed in the possibility of the Southern States achieving their independence until it heard the news of the disastrous retreat from the lines of the Chickahominy; and Major-Gen. George B. McClellan will indubitably be held responsible by history for the result of that humiliating campaign, and the subsequent change in the sympathies of the world.

THE END

٢

www.ingramcontent.com/pod-product-compliance
Lightning Source LLC
Chambersburg PA
CBHW020903230426
43666CB00008B/1296